From Montaigne
to Montaigne

From Montaigne to Montaigne

Claude Lévi-Strauss

Edited by Emmanuel Désveaux

Translated by Robert Bononno

Introduction by Peter Skafish

 University of Minnesota Press
Minneapolis / London

The University of Minnesota Press gratefully acknowledges financial support
for the publication of this book from the Centre national du livre.

The University of Minnesota Press recognizes that the language and approach
of Claude Lévi-Strauss's anthropological research are not always appropriate
today. This is true of passages in this book, especially in "Ethnography: A
Revolutionary Science," a speech he delivered in 1937. In order to provide
accurate historical documents, we reprinted Lévi-Strauss's speeches here in
their original form while also acknowledging that some of this language is no
longer acceptable.

Every effort was made to obtain permission to reproduce material in this book.
If any proper acknowledgment has not been included here, we encourage
copyright holders to notify the publisher.

Published by the University of Minnesota Press
111 Third Avenue South, Suite 290
Minneapolis, MN 55401-2520
http://www.upress.umn.edu

ISBN 978-1-5179-0637-5 (hc)
ISBN 978-1-5179-0638-2 (pb)

A Cataloging-in-Publication record for this book is available from the Library
of Congress.

Printed in the United States of America on acid-free paper

The University of Minnesota is an equal-opportunity educator and employer.

25 24 23 22 21 20 19   10 9 8 7 6 5 4 3 2 1

Contents

From Montaigne to Montaigne

Introduction

Structuralist Relativism for the Changes of the Cosmos

Peter Skafish

September reverses and the equinoxes flip
Winter slides into fall . . .
They spring back and fall forward
—*Gastr del Sol, "The Seasons Reverse"*

Claude Lévi-Strauss once expressed that it would bring him joy to cross the line, the uncrossable line over which one can fully communicate with an animal. The enlightened but surrealistic genius and perennial yet undead patriarch of a whole discipline made this remark (which provides the epigraph to Loyer's recent biography of him) late in the autumn of his centenarian life, explaining that only by attaining "this unattainable goal" could he overcome the pain of "knowing that I will never be able to find out of what the matter and structure of the universe is made."[1]

The passing of a full half-century since the Anglophone reception of Lévi-Strauss and structuralism—*Tristes Tropiques*, *Anthropologie Structurale*, and *La Pensée Sauvage* were translated in 1961, 1963, and 1966, and their critical assessment occurred largely from then through the next decade—has done little to change the significance that readers today will attach to the anthropologist's desire to connect with animals. In spite of how common it is for anthropologists to esteem Lévi-Strauss as their ancestral founder, the English-language interpretation of his work is at low tide, the sense of what it says largely frozen in standard pedagogical readings and the great critiques made decades ago by the (often so-called) poststructuralists.[2] This intimidatingly demiurgic author of some of the most fundamental and most advanced concepts not only of anthropology but of the other humanities and social sciences—the intellect that dreamed up not just alliance theory, structural analysis, symbolic efficacy, and the *bricoleur* but also the floating signifier, the canonical formula, the logic of the sensible, and transformation groups—*that* intellect, *Claude Lévi-Strauss* (!), is still often imagined, even sympathetically, to be the remote scientist who believed that he could imprison all meaning in a narrow gamut of semantic oppositions that are supposed to be the mind's structures; who conceived of the manifestation of those structures in kinship and language as what make humans irrevocably human, that is, cultural rather than natural; and who at the same time attempted to impose limits on culture's inevitable upending of human essences by surreptitiously anchoring it in nature, through locating the incest prohibition and thus sexual difference in biology;

postulating an original social state innocent of writing and technics; and sheltering it from the rough play of signifiers and their unending deviation of significations. No doubt "Lévi-Strauss" wished, it will be said, that an animal could convey to him the ultimate secret of the universe, as he suffered from a particularly severe case of the European will to know the ultimate foundation of things. . . .

As long as that sad caricature of the anthropologist stands, the projects of each of the pair of lectures that *From Montaigne to Montaigne* comprises—the revolutionary ethnological science of the first, 1937, lecture and the unlimited anthropological relativism of the other, from 1992—will seem quite dubious, and of merely historical interest. For the radical value of Lévi-Strauss's version of that but seemingly reactionary science will become apparent only by refusing to let the old criticisms eclipse his thought and the reflections of it created by some of its satellites. Among the many suddenly novel aspects of his oeuvre that then come to light are the at once speculative and critical concept of relativism by which Lévi-Strauss sought to displace the modern variation of thought from its position as the measure of all others and to help bring out the unacknowledged philosophies asleep within them.

That there could be such critical force in of all things relativism will seem improbable even to anthropologists who were never persuaded by the deconstruction of Lévi-Strauss, and this is largely because the project of *Thought in the Wild* (as *La Pensée Sauvage* ought now to be translated) no longer seems subversive.[3] In 1962, more than a decade prior to Paul Feyerabend's *Against Method* and well more than two before Donna Haraway's *Simians,*

Cyborgs, and Women and Bruno Latour's *We Have Never Been Modern*, came the most systematic book by the anthropologist since *The Elementary Structures of Kinship*, along with its claim that there is as much logic and reason in the crudest and most "primitive" of indigenous thought as the most advanced modern science. That thesis and the case that Lévi-Strauss made for it in his analyses of the rich logic of the concrete at work in indigenous classificatory systems cannot shock a time in which reason has little prestige, but it was virtually scandalous at the moment when American technoscience was newly ascendant and the cultural authority of the enlightened French had not yet fallen. Just as alarming then was Lévi-Strauss's polemical argument that Sartre's conception of humanity as historical in its being is no more than a parochial European fantasy that collapses in the face of the diffidence toward the fire of historical change of Amerindian "cold societies." It might be thought that the relativist disparagement of such an unquestioned premise of *critique* would perturb today's academics where the same treatment of science does not, but that would require them to recognize that they function within a variation of thought that is only one among others and that its universality can be put at risk. Even when it is recalled that *Thought in the Wild* preceded by four years Foucault's *The Order of Things* and Lacan's *Écrits* and inaugurated structuralism as an intellectual ethos concerned with anonymous structures and differential relations rather than subjects, their identities through time, and other midcentury concepts that remain constitutive of the humanities and social sciences, it is nevertheless felt that there is no encompassing modern way of thinking left that Lévi-Strauss would have the power to disrupt.

Lévi-Strauss's brief commentary on Montaigne reveals, however, that the anthropologist retains an immense capacity to expose and then destabilize our location in thought. The lecture may be among the lightest and most incidental of the essays and talks edited into posthumous books since his death in 2009, but as Emmanuel Désveaux notes in the introduction to the original French volume, it connects into and clarifies two other pieces of writing on Montaigne that Lévi-Strauss published around the same time: "Montaigne in America," a brief article that appeared in the Italian newspaper *La Republicca*, and "Rereading Montaigne," a chapter of the last book in the series known as the "minor" *Mythologiques, The Story of Lynx*. Each of these texts offers a different variation of an argument for the enduring relevance of Montaigne's case in "De Cannibalis" for the humanity of the Tupi encountered a few decades before its writing by European colonists and for the barbarism of the latter: "Montaigne in America" stresses that the Tupi's influence on Montaigne's view of the civility of living close to nature in turn significantly shaped European philosophy, including that behind the French Revolution, while *Lynx*'s "Rereading Montaigne" dwells on how their strong influence on the essayist's invention of relativism requires that they also be credited with his rehabilitation of skepticism. "Return to Montaigne" adds that the essayist offers relativism as one of three ways of reckoning with the consequences of the Tupi's existence, each of which effectively corresponds to both an instance of Enlightenment thought and a way that anthropology has been done: the other two anticipate Diderot's understanding of a state of nature of which indigenous Americans would be the remaining expression and Rousseau's conception of an essential society, the principles of which can be discerned in the most primitive of cultures. Montaigne's relativism, by contrast, limits itself to recognizing that there are reasons for every custom and that the "reason" behind one's own is unlikely to explain them. As Désveaux remarks, this affirmation of Montaigne as the philosophical precursor of anthropology and relativism as its principle is a marked departure from Lévi-Strauss's more frequent ascription of those roles to Rousseau and the *promeneur*'s ideal of a primordial social state.[4] In his winter, the anthropologist forgets a bit about the possible invariants of humanity and perceives it primarily through its variations.

If taken by itself, that change will not seem significant enough to turn Lévi-Strauss and structuralism into revolutionary thought. When situated in its immediate and then broader place in his work, however, this shift abruptly attains such importance. Like *The Story of Lynx* and "Montaigne in America," "Return to Montaigne" falls around a year (1992) about which a master disciple of the Americas could have only felt disgust, and the three texts together contain a barely veiled rebuke of the commemoration of Colombus's invasion as a discovery. As it was the full book that he published the year prior as well as the final volume of the three-decade *Mythologiques* cycle, Lévi-Strauss struck hardest in *The Story of Lynx*, declaring the indigenous thought expressed in the myths of both continents to be philosophy, and philosophy equal to if not superior to that of Europe for having difference as its speculative principle.[5] That astonishing statement was effectively intended to elevate Amerindian thought above not only most philosophy but also the sciences that partake in its metaphysics of identity: nonclassical knowledges such as quantum physics are said to be alone among their peers in detecting the sorts of double, perceptually impossible beings, like Schrödinger's cat, that are a matter of course in myth, and it is implied that structural anthropology first learned of differential relations from that and other forms of native thought. The relativism sketched in "Return to Montaigne" thus turns out to extend all the way to the metaphysical foundation that most modern, if not European, thought imagines to be its own, and to confront it with the pervasive reality of an alien (an-)*arche*.

.   .   .

Of course it must be asked if Lévi-Strauss's thought as a whole indeed leads to such an extreme, almost bottomless relativism, or whether his wishes late in life exceeded even his wealth of intellectual means. Much can be found in that estate to recommend against the first possibility, from its unrenounced Rousseauean inheritance to its vast investment in the nature/culture distinction to its promotion of structure as standard intellectual currency. Yet it is precisely a structuralism that is inherently capable of displacing fundamental modern concepts and thereby decolonizing thought that is both attributed to Lévi-Strauss by two of his most inventive descendants—Philippe Descola and Eduardo Viveiros de Castro—and practiced by them on its basis. As their work is the most influential of the remaining uses of the anthropologist's thought, their interpretations of it have become almost inseparable from any response that might be given to the question.[6]

This proposition may seem even more bewildering than those raised before, as that pair has engaged together in a relentless critique of nature and culture that begins with the undue role that Lévi-Strauss accorded the distinction in the thought of the Amazonian and other lowland South American peoples to which their work is devoted. Both Descola and Viveiros de Castro argued in their initial, respective ethnographic works *In the Society of Nature* and *From the Enemy's Point of View* that Lévi-Strauss was quite wrong in *Thought in the Wild* to treat the long serial analogies between nature and culture sometimes present in indigenous classification and myth as almost the essence of so-called primitive if not all human thought, as some of his exemplars of these come from peoples in the Amazon basin who in practice make no such distinction. By Descola's reckoning, Lévi-Strauss misconstrued certain correspondences drawn in their thought as A:B::C:D analogies by which social relations are modeled on the links between natural species because the animals and plants that he placed in the natural series were already thoroughly inscribed in such human social relations, whether of politics, kinship, or knowledge. Viveiros de Castro adds that such "totemic" analogies, as they are called in *Thought in the Wild*, were further exaggerated in importance when Lévi-Strauss conceived of them there as the primordial means, in use since the Neolithic era, by which the transindividual human intellect makes (metaphoric) signs from nature and thus introduces intellectual discontinuities into it, and opposed them to sacrificial rituals that he characterized as vain attempts by individuals to establish (metonymic) continuities between the terms in each series and thereby reenter the undistinguished condition of nature. This distinction between totemism and sacrifice holds only so long in lowland South America, Viveiros de Castro contends, as ritual cannibalism and other sacrificial techniques instead aim at overcoming the discontinuities that are there thought to exist between quasi-*natural* species in order that one might enter into the human *cultural* continuum to which they all still belong and thereby attain their perspectives. Thus, prior to their systematic displacements of nature and culture in their major theoretical works *Beyond Nature and Culture* and *Cannibal Metaphysics*, Descola and Viveiros de Castro had already left the binary opposition of all binary oppositions in bad shape.[7]

Yet, to both of them, Lévi-Strauss' structuralism, especially after *Thought in the Wild*, is something else and far more than a sprawling analytic project that has the reproduction of that distinction as its sole design, and each builds their own work from a version of his thought. To Descola, the nature/culture distinction increasingly became after *Thought in the Wild* a semantic shortcut by which Lévi-Strauss could find the many, more subtle contrasts inventoried in the *Mythologies* and that also concealed a *monistic* understanding of nature that arguably first surfaced in *The Elementary Structures* and had become by the 1970s one of his espoused principles.[8] In a lecture delivered in New York in 1972 and later published as "Structuralism and Ecology," the anthropologist countered the frequent criticism that structuralism is an idealism by demonstrating that it accounts with startling accuracy for how the permutations of the structures of myths are determined as much by their sociotechnical and ecological milieus as by the contrastive operations of the mind. The celebrated analysis of Heiltsuk and Tŝilhqot'in myths by which he there makes the case for the ecological origin of the role in them of motifs such as shells and horns is followed by an argument that the reason that the human mind readily thinks with such sensible objects is that their opposable qualities (such as concave and convex) are already homologous with and perhaps even inscribed in the differentiated cellular "structures" of the sense organs and the brain. In his opus *Beyond Nature and Culture*, Descola finds in this nondualist structuralism the basis for his account of animist and other extramodern cosmologies that do not distinguish between nature and culture, and addresses in the process a problem acknowledged but left unresolved in *Thought in the Wild*. Lévi-Strauss there postulates that quasi-Kantian schemas must mediate between general structures of the mind and specific practices but says little about what those schemas might be. Descola proposes that they are cognitive dispositions that lead every human being to identify entities as being in essence either continuous or discontinuous with itself by evaluating whether they have or do not have (a) a subjective consciousness, or "interiority," and (b) a body, or "physicality," like those that are its own. By making the basis of that pair of queries immediate aspects of human apperception and conceiving of each of the four possible answers ("animism," "totemism," "analogism," and "naturalism") as the foundation of a corresponding swathe of the diversity of human practices, he is able to offer a structuralist account of the cognitive genesis of extramodern practices that does not impose on them nature/culture dualism but gives it a status no greater than their own governing ontological distributions.[9] In fact, Descola takes this monism so far that he refuses to concede that there is a reality of primary qualities to which the modern, naturalist schema would have privileged access and the others only erroneous representations. He dares, that is, to relativize both the sciences and their universe.

In contrast, Viveiros de Castro practices a hyperdualist structuralism, which he most fully finds even later in the anthropologist's corpus. This is the work of a sort of trickster Lévi-Strauss who increasingly forwards intellectual proposals that contradict the firmest of his prior conclusions as the major and minor *Mythologies* progress. The most significant of these may be, the Brazilian anthropologist argues, *The Story of Lynx*'s characterization of Amerindian myth as a collective philosophy of the "perpetual disequilibrium" of "unstable dualisms."[10] Lévi-Strauss ends the final of the *Mythologies* and his very last book with that formula in part to account for why one of the most puzzling series of myths in the cycle has twins as its core obsession and conceives of them not (as Indo-European mythology does) as rare identical beings but as irreducibly different. Such myths, he says, take the dualities that form their structures as their object and do so because they register that humans and everything else that is are also constituted by bipartite contrasts, such as those between Indian and Other and sky and earth, which can be temporarily but never ultimately equated: while twins may initially suggest that human thought can resolve and eliminate duality, their disparity is a reminder that equivalence is the case only with distinct beings and therefore is subsequent to difference.

In Viveiros de Castro's estimation, Lévi-Strauss arrived at this idea because he was on the verge of understanding the Brazilian's own view that beings as such have in Amazonia an equivocal status—each of them is predator or prey, human or animal, culture or nature, same or other depending on which of the others is perceiving it—and structuralism gave him a sense of this effectively ontological relativism because it is a translation of it. Perhaps the strongest confirmation of this consonance between the two anthropologists is that Lévi-Strauss attests to this "perspectivist" and predatory metaphysics of equivocation, as Viveiros de Castro calls it, in the many points of the *Mythologies* that reckon with its effect on kinship. In contrast with the custom that prevails in most kinship systems, those in lowland South America often use marriage alliance not to connect the group to other groups but to keep it within itself, to which corresponds the equally unusual habit of naming affines ("in-laws") created by alliance as cognates (brothers-in-law are called "cousins") and outsiders as affines (trade partners and enemies in war are called "brothers-in-law"). Viveiros de Castro's explanation of this anomaly in the practice and nomenclature of kinship is that any collective displaying it is not initially an integral unity that then enters into relations of social exchange through marriage but a lacerated, exposed pole in other, more primary relations of cosmic exchange (warfare, hunting, and shamanism) with other human and animal collectives in which the aim on both sides is to incorporate and transform the other into the same. In a collective that exists outside itself among inhospitable others that threaten to cannibalize and redefine it, one's relatives through marriage are tenuous prizes won from those enemy peoples and at the same time alien representatives of them that are thus best imagined as "blood," while unintegrated foreigners are open enemies little different from the ambivalent "in-laws" into which they may be converted (if the same is not done to oneself). That relations as such in Amazonia are frequently in this way kin and/or nonkin, friend and/or enemy, and internal and/or external obviously undermines the equation of kinship with humanity and society made in *The Elementary Structures*, but Viveiros de Castro offers in *Cannibal Metaphysics* an audacious account of how the *Mythologies* nevertheless describe this primacy of equivocation in their many analyses of myths in which cannibal brothers-in-law both persecute and abet heroes, affines are simultaneously consanguines, humans change into animals, and every other sort of being proves to be the same as and the opposite of itself.[11]

Such precise depictions of perspectivism can come from Lévi-Strauss, by this interpretation, because both his concepts and his method are originally native to it. Whether abstractions like the continuous and discontinuous or tangibles like the raw and the cooked, the classic structuralist dualities are often translations of the pairs of incompossible predicates that beings simultaneously hold in Amazonia, and Lévi-Strauss's way of uncovering them with analogies between the different complexes of relations, or structures, that they form from myth to myth is effectively the native procedure for gaining some control over both those equivocations and the Other (per the well-known interspecies example, understanding that one must be prey for the jaguar as the peccary is to oneself enables one to turn the situation back on the jaguar). Holding that view about the source of structural analysis is what leads Viveiros de Castro to draw such an analogy to elucidate perspectivism—that the unity of nature is to the plurality of cultures in modern thought as the uniformity of human cultures is to the heterogeneity of collectives–species in indigenous thought—while claiming that device to be, in principle, no less Amerindian than structuralist. And to think that, like its perspectivist model, such an anthropological comparison of structures succeeds only if it exposes the disaccord between the familiar dualities by which it is conducted and the alien dualities that it reveals—and that the former, modern concepts thus travel poorly, unless they transform.

.   .   .

Viveiros de Castro's and Descola's interpretations thus put one before the rich, often neglected parts of Lévi-Strauss's oeuvre in which their own structuralist relativisms are authorized and already at work. Yet there is no need to leave texts as canonical as *Tristes Tropiques* and the essays gathered in *Structural Anthropology, Volume 2* to witness contemporary "ontology" prepared in plain view.

It was just before the appearance of the former text, in

the high summer of his life, that the anthropologist published his famed report on racism for UNESCO, "Race and History," and proposed to counter the ideas of cultural inequality that subtended and were already replacing biological racism with a "theory of relativity generalized quite differently from Einstein's [in that] it would be applicable at the same time to the physical sciences and social sciences" (!).[12] In a discussion that remains to this day underappreciated, Lévi-Strauss argues that the almost indisputable impression that the West then gave of being the forefront of human progress depends on its imposition of its kind of technological development as the criterion for the determination, as that inevitably relegates other cultures and their incommensurate goods—Taoist thought and its body techniques, Islam and its ideal of solidarity between all aspects of human life—to the middle or rear.[13] Such a valuation appears as certain as the trajectory and speed of bodies do when it is forgotten that they are functions of the position of the observer, and relative when it is recognized that a passenger on a train will regard both the speed and the length of a passing train as inversely greater or smaller in relation to each other depending on whether this other train is traveling in the same or opposite direction. One's location in one's culture and vis-à-vis others and theirs is like that of this rail passenger, Lévi-Strauss continues, as one cannot exit one's position for an overview and thus ends up perceiving cultures that develop in the opposite direction as unintelligible:

> It is possible to accumulate far more information about
> a train moving along a parallel path at a speed similar

to ours (one can see the faces of the passengers, count them, etc.) than about a train that passes us, or which we pass at very great speed, or which seems to us to get shorter because it goes in another direction. At the limit, it goes so fast that we can only keep a confused impression of it from which the very signs of speed are absent; it is reduced to a temporary blurring of the field of vision. It is no longer a train, it *signifies* nothing anymore.[14]

As easy as it is to assume that this explanation of the incomprehensibility of incommensurate cultures is an attempt to establish a universal principle by which to recognize and order them, the mistake in that is that Lévi-Strauss not only opposes his account to the culturalist racism with which such liberal projects are enmeshed but also treats the West's conception of technoscientific modernity as the apex of humanity as almost the paradigm of that racism. Almost immediately after enunciating his concept of relativity, he clarifies that it is not idle academic conjecture but an instrument for combating the recognition of the purported superiority of the West that was then prevailing among the world's societies.[15] In this, Lévi-Strauss effectively verges on Anabel Quijano's later idea that the postcolonial political order rests on the "coloniality" that persists after decolonization, the pervasive feeling that every variation of human existence besides that of the white, technologized moderns pathetically languishes while they achieve unheard-of levels of efficacy, vitality, and autonomy.[16] In light of the anthropologist's unanticipated articulation of such a subtle conception of race, the analogy by which he uses physical relativity to define cultural relativity ought to be read as subversive of the natural sciences and thus too of the exclusive right of moderns to decide the truth about the cosmos and the differences between its human inhabitants.

That this relativism is in this way *ontological* is attested to by other essays from the same period. Another that is reprinted in *Structural Anthropology, Volume 2*, "Scientific Criteria in the Social and Human Disciplines," distinguishes anthropology and the other human sciences from the social sciences by their respective orientations to their Euroamerican provenance: unlike economics, political science, and much sociology, anthropology and its sibling disciplines are said to be concerned with the outside rather than the inside of European thought, to think along a centrifugal trajectory, and to reach thereby a "point of view of immanence" rather than that of the false "transcendence" entailed when one's culture is imagined to be a "separate, legitimately self-contained universe."[17] As much as Lévi-Strauss draws that metaphysical distinction in order to define the epistemological conditions of anthropology, he does not hesitate to acknowledge the ontological implications. About the plurality of worlds, past and present, studied by the human and social sciences, he asks

> Of all these worlds, which is the right one? And if all are (or none is), where is the subject of the social and human sciences located, behind or in front of them? The difference between these sciences reflects the alternatives which torment them [. . .]: either to favor one of the worlds in order to gain a hold over it; or to call them all into question for the benefit of a common essence

which remains to be discovered; or of a single universe, which if it is really unique, will unfailingly come to merge with that of the hard sciences.[18]

His responses to those questions in other texts diverge along the same lines traced before, splitting between, on the one hand, his reliable, diurnal affirmations of anthropology as a science that uncovers beneath the variants of human thought its structural invariants and their points of coincidence with the universe; and, on the other, his unexpected, nocturnal asides that structural anthropology is little more than a variation of its objects of study and that its and their structures are just a few in the endless series that make up what is instead a pluriverse.[19]

As incompatible as that pair of answers may be, both are indeed as unsparing of modern thought as is claimed. The denial of universality to many of the unquestioned concepts that hold together much twentieth-century philosophy and even critical theory begins at this time to enter the decades-long crest of *The Origin of Table Manners*'s indictment of anthropocentrism, *The Naked Man*'s critique of humanism and the subject, *The Jealous Potter*'s rejection of modern sexuality as the model of all others, and *Look, Listen, Read*'s finishing off of the idea of a postfigurative aesthetic telos. Yet one need not read outside the dog days of Lévi-Strauss to witness philosophical ideas expiring under their searing light. The celebrated case for deciding to live as, with, and for humanity and against nihilist individualism in the final pages of *Tristes Tropiques* is not based on European philosophy and its subject, which are declared to be "myths" that a coming anthropology "will deal with no more gently than traditional sociology does."[20] The alternatives that he proposes, however, are not the tedious work of the social sciences and their modern savant but the serene pleasure of another kind of thought and its endlessly diverse practitioners: that of humans pondering their own essence(s) by way of the sensible, nonhuman stuff of the universe—the animals, flowers, and minerals to which such thought in the wild is immanent—that preceded and will endure long after the extinction of the last of those humans and their worlds.[21] The comparative anthropology promulgated throughout the text does not get the last word, and its execution there through concrete, aesthetic means confirms that it was to Lévi-Strauss no more than an instance of this other sort of contrastive thinking and as subordinate as it to the Earth. This is why the feature-length comparative "mental tracking shot" by which *Tristes Tropiques* covers its author's long itinerary of Paris → São Paolo → Caduveo → Bororo → Nambikwara → Tupi-Kawahib → Imperial Rome → Paris → Martinique → New York → Taxila can sometimes linger over features of European intellectual geography like French rationalism and Marxism while nevertheless diminishing their size on the broader pensive landscape.[22]

.   .   .

It seems that one would be right to see in this period of Lévi-Strauss the iridescent bloom of his youthful declaration that ethnology is revolutionary thought. At the moment when Fanon, Sartre, and Arendt invented critiques of colonialism only rarely alluded to by a subsequent generation of philosophers, Lévi-Strauss was not only denouncing in parallel its and modernity's violence but doing so through the sort of interested use of research into indigenous thought that he claims, in "Ethnography: A Revolutionary Science," flares in influence around moments like 1789 France and 1917 Russia (as well as, it could be added, 1968 Earth). In spite of the distance from politics that he would often subsequently maintain, Lévi-Strauss was undertaking by the 1950s such a critical science in response to and support of the era's anticolonial movements.

Yet that anthropology was obviously not in practice revolutionary by most definitions, as it did not and could not undo the vast imbalances of power between the countries of its practitioners and the peoples it studied. If some worth nevertheless remains in Lévi-Strauss's claim to radicality, it lies in its pertinence to his descendants' and their opponents' claims about the relevance to critique of contemporary structuralism. Viveiros de Castro too has linked a certain indigenous turn in anthropology to revolutionary politics (those of 1968 and today's incipient green revolution), and both he and Descola have called their work the decolonization of thought in part because it provides concrete intellectual resources to the ongoing struggles of South American indigenous groups against land and resource extraction. At the same time, that pair have been accused (usually on the flimsiest of ad hominems) of reinforcing the longstanding asymmetry between settler and native intellectual agency by emphasizing traditional indigenous thought to the neglect of its hybrid and contemporary versions. That criticism is already based on a thorough misunderstanding of the provincializing character of their projects, and it may be further weakened by the young Lévi-Strauss's connecting of indigenous ethnology to revolution. It is worth considering whether that association is given new meaning by the coincidence of the ontological turn with a group of events that have brought upheaval to Euroamerican modernity: the emergence of a multipolar political order; the reattainment of cosmological and intellectual authority by Islamic, Chinese, African, and other variations of thought; the social–economic acceleration being brought on by digital technology and artificial intelligence; and climate change. The sibling Americanists are well known to have addressed the conditions of the ecological crisis by counterposing cosmologies with no concept of but great respect for "nature" to the modernity that has the idea while devastating the thing, but they have also transformed structuralism into a means of exposing the irreducibility of the above and all other variations of thought to that of modernity; of situating the posthuman condition that is being engendered in certain moderns by technology as only one among the dilemmas faced by a greater panhumanity; and of working through (rather than denying) the question of the essence of modern thought raised by the decline in North Atlantic power. As the ecological crisis renders the other events into interfused aspects of a truly planetary emergency, Lévi-Straussian structuralism may prove to be among the few conceptual resources that can address the situation of humans as a whole and to do so *by virtue of its engagement with and redeployment of indigenous thought*. It will be largely for indigenous thinkers the likes of Coulthard, Rivera-Cusicanqui, and Kopenawa to determine its successes and failures at that, but the chances are low that the balance sheet will near red.

Lévi-Strauss's prospects at such a future for now depend on how—on *whether*—one wants him to be read, as the version of him presented here will remain unrecognizable to certain of his onetime readers despite the clear evidence for his engagement with ontological and critical issues. That the present portrait can still seem implausible stems less from the judgments of some that he is deserving of only the most dismissive engagement than from the experience of others that his texts confound the most cultivated readerly expectations. Even as the long cycle of Lévi-Strauss's thought requires an effectively philosophical apprenticeship to be followed, he was decidedly not a philosopher and yet also neither a philosopher wearing a scientific mask nor an antiphilosopher opposing philosophical truth and thus often ungraspable by even ungrasping ways of reading.[23] As a kind, he was something other still, a quietly outlandish thinker who can only be heard by an ear as sharp as his to alterity.

In his inaugural lecture at the Collège de France, Lévi-Strauss demonstrates the structuralist method for determining if myths and other phenomena are variants of each other through the example of the coappearance of incest and riddles in Occidental and Amerindian thought. The sort of "question without answer" posed to Oedipus by the Sphinx is ubiquitous in Indo-European myths but nonexistent in those of the Americas outside the exceptional few that likewise concern incest. For the presence of that pair in each case to be more than fortuitous, he continues, there must be myths in both that couple in homologous fashion inversions of both "the hero who mis-uses sexual intercourse" and of the riddle as pure question, which indeed are found in some European and in many Amerindian tales of a "chaste hero who abstains from sex" and has "*an answer for which there is no question.*"[24] In establishing this transformation, Lévi-Strauss also in-advertently offers profiles of the persona and the form of thought that even comprehending readers are vexed to encounter in *The Mythologies* and the works that follow: answer upon answer to unstated questions, and a frigid academic who could suspect philosophy, as he verges on doing in the lecture, of being perversion of the same order as both "the solved riddle" and "incest" in that it "brings together terms meant to remain separate: the son is joined with the mother, the brother with the sister, *in the same way that the answer succeeds, against all expectations, in refinding its question.*"[25] In contrast with cunning philos-ophers who raise unanswerable but endlessly addressable questions, Lévi-Strauss (by this possible unconscious ad-mission) would be a naïve thinker with endless, unasked for answers—"an innocent," he says, "who does not even know how to ask questions."[26]

To learn from such a guileless mind, perhaps we have to reverse background and figure in the already inverted approach to reading applied to philosophers by looking for the answers rather than the questions—for statements so transparent that they become enigmas upon scrutiny—and then find or imagine their missing interrogative mates. In the present lecture, we would then discover that the myths of the incestuous hero and his virginal alter also respectively concern the anomalous climactic conditions of eternal winter—"which the hero dispels when he solves the riddles"—and permanent summer, the hold over the other seasons of which is broken by the celibate's discovery of his question.[27] The anthropologist turns out to be saying (contrary to what he had just implied) that it is by trying either to eliminate difference through incest or to deny it with abstinence that it is returned to power and restores change. Thus the answers of the degeneracy of the philosopher and the asexuality of the mythologist are compounded by those of the rightness of their breachings of the order of things and of the benefit to climate, animals, and humans. Or, apropos the quandary of how to follow an innocent thinker: just as the philosopher had best sometimes come to the answer, so the anthropologist must eventually give in to the advances of the question. Lévi-Strauss finally relented—to the disequilibria of dualities—as some of us are deciding to enter counternatural, countermodern unions with our relatives of the Earth.

From Montaigne
to Montaigne

Lévi-Strauss and the Diffusionist Moment

Emmanuel Désveaux

Presented more than half a century apart, the two talks brought together in this book reflect one another: they bracket a very long cycle of public speaking by one of the most celebrated French anthropologists of the twentieth century.[1] In all likelihood, the first talk was given in January 1937 and the second in April 1992. The year was special for Lévi-Strauss in that it celebrated the five hundredth anniversary of European arrival in America and the four hundredth year after the death of Montaigne, both of which had a played a large role in his life.

During that same year, my essay "Un itinéraire de Lévi-Strauss—De Rousseau à Montaigne," appeared in the review *Critique*.[2] This was a commentary inspired by a reading of his *Histoire de Lynx*, which had appeared the previous autumn.[3] We find Lévi-Strauss moving from a kind of exchange-based harmony that would have been acceptable to Rousseau to a much more disenchanted view of human nature, synonymous with the steadfast melancholy found in Montaigne. This would situate the origin of his anthropological beliefs in *The Elementary Structures of Kinship*. In doing so, we would highlight a shared element of exegesis, one maintained by the author throughout his life. However, we would be mistaken to follow that line of inquiry. It is true that at the time the 1937 conference, only recently discovered in the archives of the Bibliothèque national de France, was unknown. Its discovery has led us to substantially revise our view of Lévi-Strauss's first steps as an anthropologist. Through this text, initially quite disconcerting, an unexpected glimpse of his thought rises to the surface: one in which he subscribed to a form of orthodox diffusionism. This being the case, to the extent that diffusionism constitutes a variant—or, rather, the matrix, as we shall see—of cultural relativism, it now seems preferable to describe Lévi-Strauss's itinerary as starting from Montaigne and ending with Montaigne, which, of course, doesn't prevent us from acknowledging the signal importance of the Rousseauian phase of his work. In fact, as will appear from the text, the 1937 conference contains the beginnings of this move.

When Lévi-Strauss left for Brazil in1935, accompanied by his wife,[4] he was invited as a professor of sociology—not as an anthropologist or ethnologist. He had made a few acquaintances in the field in Paris and done some reading on exotic ethnography, but not much more. This is all the more striking when we consider that his reading, and his personal encounters, already displayed strong leanings toward Americanism, along with Jean de Léry, his sixteenth-century ancestor, and Robert Lowie, who helped him settle in New York seven years later.[5] In reality, it was in São Paolo, in the ferment preceding his expeditions, that Lévi-Strauss began studying anthropology seriously (or ethnology, or ethnography, three terms that I'll provisionally treat as near synonyms, as Lévi-Strauss himself did), a subject in which he was largely self-taught.[6] It's true that at the time, in comparison to what was happening elsewhere, French universities had little to offer in the subject, with the exception of a handful of brilliant but isolated individuals such as Marcel Mauss and Marcel Granet. Human geography, as taught by Paul Vidal de la Blache, who enjoyed tremendous prestige at the time, dominated the field through a comprehensive understanding of the world and, in so doing, held back the growth of the discipline. Anthropology was being studied in the United States, Great Britain, and Germany, and it is likely that successive deliveries of *American Anthropologist*, the *Journal of the Royal Anthropological Institute*, and *Anthropos* at the library of the University of São Paolo played a crucial role in jump-starting the exiled young professor's knowledge of the leading topics and methodological rudiments of the discipline. However, in the years 1920 to 1930 a major debate roiled the field, which the neophyte anthropologist could hardly have avoided. It pitted two visions of cultural diversity against one another, sometimes with considerable asperity—with functionalism serving as the arbiter between them. A slender volume, published in New York in 1927, to which the leading intellects of the time contributed, provides a highly suggestive image of this polemic.[7] It turns out that both camps had recourse to the concept of diffusion but didn't assign it the same function.

The first perspective represents the exacerbated face of evolutionism. According to this theory, whenever a human group progresses in some way, for example, through the adoption of pottery, this is necessarily the result of importation. There is only one single source of human innovation, namely Ancient Egypt and the West, understood broadly, from which all progress was diffused throughout the world, with greater or lesser speed and success, of course, which explains the backward nature of certain populations. The opposing argument pleaded the cause of co-invention. From this perspective, there are several "civilizational" sites, all of which are centers of creativity and from which innovations, as well as cultural traits, *diffuse* regionally—and sometimes across whole continents. One clarification is necessary, however. At the height of the polemic, the first position could have been qualified as "diffusionist" by its opponents to the extent that, in practice, from its perspective *everything* is eventually diffused.[8] However, to the extent that this position was totally beholden to evolutionism, the term diffusionism was ultimately reserved for the opposite viewpoint, in which diffusion becomes a true theoretical object. In this case the process consists, given a cultural trait observed by the ethnographer—or revealed by the archeologist—in not assuming a priori that which occurs through endogenesis and that which comes from outside, which is derivative or borrowed. *Diffusion*, as such, becomes an index and not the shameful stain of creative inadequacy. It is torn from the obsession with progress and originary location, inviting us to examine space in order to identify the extension and limits of the distribution of the components of a culture. Seen in this light, diffusionism has several consequences. It entails a kind of indexation of cultural traits, that is, a sifting of ethnographic material, which obscures the distinction between infrastructures and superstructures. Not only does it enable us to serenely imagine a plurality of sites from which "innovations" emerge but goes so far as to question the equivalence between two forms of "progress," to the extent that lack of contact between them can be established. As Spinden noted, the status and implications of agriculture may differ, depending on whether it is based on wheat, as was the case in the Middle East, on rice, as was the case in the Far East, on corn, as was the case in Mesoamerica, or on manioc, as was the case in the American lowlands.[9] In this sense, diffusionism becomes a form of analysis capable of accounting for phenomena in all their complexity—but also capable of weakening the bases of historical materialism.

It is in this context that we should situate the talk given by Lévi-Strauss in January 1937 before an audience of socialist and pacifist members of the CGT.[10] He made his presentation during a brief stay in Paris during the winter of 1936–37, between the two ethnographic trips discussed in *Tristes Tropiques*, that is, between his journey to meet the Caduveo and Bororo peoples and the primitivist mirage evinced by the Nambikwara.[11] I'll return below to his lengthy introduction, in which he discusses the "revolutionary" nature of ethnography. For the time being, we should bear in mind that such a claim served as an attack on any form of evolutionist logic, and specifically to promote what has been described as diffusionism.

Lévi-Strauss first describes the term "primitive" applied

to traditional exotic populations. These are not primitive because they are closer to humanity's origins, which is to say backwards in our terms, but simply because they have not undergone the kinds of developments that obscure their nature. Which is why they have intrinsic value. We know that Lévi-Strauss would remain faithful to this belief until he wrote the four volumes of *Mythologiques*. But the typically diffusionist element lies in the claim that these societies were able to develop in parallel, which is to say completely differently, to those that characterized the past of our own societies. He expands this idea by criticizing the evolutionist theory's principal claims, namely, the belief that advanced peoples are unlike primitive peoples and, much more dangerous in his eyes (given his primitivist inclination, it is easy to see why), the postulate of a unilinearity in human evolution, by which every culture necessarily goes through the same stages as those that have gone before it. Presenting a number of examples, some borrowed from physical anthropology, Lévi-Strauss exposes the inanity of this way of seeing, evoking the field of technology, considered in and of itself or in direct engagement with sociology. The chronology that leads from the age of cut and polished stone to the Bronze Age, followed by the Iron Age, cannot be applied to Africa, where we move directly from the Stone Age to the Iron Age. The pursuit of large mammals, which assumes broad cooperation, cannot have the same social implications as the hunt for small animals. The same is true of agriculture: there are forms in which a handful of edible species are planted around the family hut and those in which much more complex agricultural methods are employed, such as livestock farming (the speaker could also have added irrigation). So, there exist almost as many hunting and agricultural practices as there are different cultures, and it makes no sense to assume that they are fundamentally identical, especially with regard to their sociological correlates; it is even worse to assume that it is possible to determine that one form inevitably preceded another.

Lévi-Strauss was by this time fully in the relativist camp. His relativism was, however, initially temporal, with an emphasis on the lengthy periods of immobility humanity had experienced, interspersed with sudden moments of acceleration. He saw a parallel between humanity's very long history and the life cycle of the individual, for whom all essential learning occurred at an advanced age. Even though the parallel may seem clumsy to us now, it's easy to see that he wanted to break down the evolutionary evidence for his audience. Abandoning a diachronic approach, he returned to the argument from a spatial perspective. And he did so by surreptitiously introducing the question of difference between nature and culture, between the laws of biology and those of universal history. If, he said, humanity had evolved somewhat like a living species ("assuming humanity had a spontaneous tendency to evolve naturally"), the distribution of cultural traits, the result of local innovation, should be highly consistent, like a harmonic juxtaposition of elements, and predictable using a mathematical model. But this isn't the case; the cartography of catalogued human phenomena turns out to be irregular. The borders between technical systems, religions, and various types of family organization initially appear to be highly random. At the same time,

Lévi-Strauss offers us a definition of culture as being a local collection of distinctive traits associated with religion,
a way of life or work, behavior, modes of family organization, institutions, and so on. This definition, which con-
solidates and levels all the components of a culture, calls to
mind that of Franz Boas (even though there is no mention
of language). We know that this will subsequently change,
especially in *The Elementary Structures of Kinship*, where
the rules of marriage become the alpha and the omega of
anthropological analysis and, therefore, of the interpretation of a given society.

The orator expounds. This is not the time to reject
evolutionism but to elaborate, as clearly as possible, the
principles of the anthropological school, which, at the
time, was the most rigorous of all and, therefore, the most
modern. In this case, it was the most orthodox version of
diffusionism that was in play. A proof of the innovative
nature of its introduction in France—which should, of
course, strengthen its appeal—was found in the fact that
its vocabulary remained unsettled. Lévi-Strauss made use
of the expression *terrains culturels* to refer to what the
Germans, at the time, called *Kulturkreise* and the Americans "cultural areas."[12] These are areas in which cultural
traits emerged before they were diffused through space
and gradually exhausted. He describes archeological work
that would validate the paradigm as clearly as possible.
Rather than paraphrase him, given the clarity of his statement, I'll quote what he himself said:

> We undertook a series of excavations in the southern
> United States, the center of five-color ceramics . . . there

we found five superimposed layers. The deepest layer contained ceramics of a single color, exactly identical to that found in the most distant area; we then found other ceramics in the other layers. This confirms the hypothesis: the five-color ceramics, which remained at the site, were the most recent, the ones that didn't have the time to spread, whereas the others are older the further they are found from the site where they were created.

In addition to a scientifically superior mechanism, orthodox diffusionism offers the advantage of converting the temporal dimension into the spatial dimension and vice versa, and does so without any loss, which no variant of evolutionism can claim to do. Yet today we would criticize this approach using the very example chosen by Lévi-Strauss himself: the model fails to explain, given some form of *intentionality* (to borrow the contemporary vocabulary credited to Alfred Gell), why a type of decoration was so admired that it was exported or adopted outside the area, or why, within a given workshop, the goods produced there became increasingly complex.[13] Why do some adapt to what comes from outside while others persist in their propensity to create new forms?

And yet, diffusionist orthodoxy cannot account for the irregularities of the spatial distribution of phenomena, irregularities that Lévi-Strauss had mentioned a few minutes earlier during his talk. But such irregularities are obviously among the symptoms of what is systematic in ethnographic material, of what creates value as well, and confers upon any culture its internal density and external articulation. In short, this represented no more than a brief postponement for the author of *Structural Anthropology*, *Totemism*, *The Savage Mind*, and the several volumes of *Mythologiques*. In this sense, it is heartening to find an entire chapter of volume three of his tetralogy in which he expresses regret for his earliest theoretical penchants.[14] Here, Lévi-Strauss criticized Thompson and his analysis of American myths, the very type of reasoning he defended thirty years earlier with respect to ceramics, namely, that a cultural trait could have a single origin and that, based on a series of concentric circles, we could follow its progression in space along a gradual scale leading to its eventual disappearance and indexed to its distance from an initial point.[15] In fact, the entire structure of the *Mythologiques* substitutes for the diffusionist model one based on logical transformation, which assumes, at a minimum, two points of reference in space and a semantic relationship of inversion between them. But it also implies the abandonment of the diachronic dimension that classical diffusionism still claimed, wrongly, to be able to control.[16]

For now, let's examine the conclusion of his talk. Taking hold of the theme of the decline of civilization propounded by Spengler, Lévi-Strauss brings up the destiny of Central Mexico. It is an example of one of the "cultural areas" touched upon earlier, probably one of the most brilliant in human history. Yet, in spite of its sophistication, it was swept away in an instant by a handful of soldiers from Spain. How can such vulnerability be explained? Quite simply by isolation. A certain amount of contact among human groups can be seen as a gauge of their respective longevity. In these final sentences he takes one further step, a premonition of his thoughts in *Race and History*: contact between peoples or cultures brings about a degree of progress because isolation generates apathy, where exchange generates movement and dynamism, excites the creative spirit, and, at the same time, stimulates social life in the cultural configuration it had previously forged for itself. This conclusion is even more surprising given that, in January 1937, Lévi-Strauss hadn't yet met the Nambikwara or lived with them or experienced, through them, the value of exchange as the best remedy for war and commerce as the surest palliative for asociality.[17] This being the case, there is a nuance here that is important to grasp: contact, intellectual exchange between two cultures, doesn't exactly mean the same thing as exchange—especially the exchange of women—on which the social order is based. But it indicates the direction. The lesson of the Nambikwara reflects a deepening more than a revelation. Lévi-Strauss's diffusionist moment paved the way; it hadn't been in vain and, in that sense, deserved to be revived.

The Two Alterities of Claude Lévi-Strauss

The talk presented by Lévi-Strauss to his CGT comrades is entitled "Ethnography: A Revolutionary Science." Lévi-Strauss, who had militated on behalf of the socialist party for years, now began to take an interest in the lives of people who were exotic, primitive, poor, neglected, living on the edge of history, and invisible to geography. But it was as if he had something to prove. In what sense were these studies relevant? And how, most critically, did they serve the revolution? The understanding of others (of course, he wasn't yet talking in these terms) goes hand in hand with a critique of one's own society. The key periods of this critical relationship to exoticism covered the sixteenth century and South America—the shadow of Montaigne, in other words—the Enlightenment and the North American noble savage—a reminiscence of Lahontan and Voltaire's *Candide*—and, finally, a reference that strikes us today as being somewhat riskier, the revolution of 1917 and the impulse it gave to ethnographic studies across the geographical immensity of the Soviet Union. Lévi-Strauss emphasized the paradox of the contemporary ethnographer. He was progressive in his own society and conservative in the field, because what he was most interested in lay precisely in the traditions, customs, and old ways of doing things. He tells us that the ethnographer really wants only one thing: that the society he is studying be spared, or be as little affected as possible by "civilization." At this point in his talk there arises a subject that would haunt Lévi-Strauss throughout his life and generations of ethnographers after him. This was the relationship between contact with the West and progress—at first material, such as the introduction of iron tools that made work easier, but moral as well, such as the disappearance of cannibalism—or, on the contrary, this same contact and the destruction of traditional cultures. Lévi-Strauss came down strongly in favor of this second option, emphasizing that the ethnographer spontaneously seeks to protect "his" populations from the harmful influence of "civilization." This led him immediately to the notion of primitivism with which we began our own commentary. There would be no point in returning to the subject other than to point out the following: the revolutionary impact of ethnography had an effect on Lévi-Strauss primarily as an intellectual. It forced him to abandon historical materialism, the determination of moments, the primacy of infrastructure and superstructure, and so on. This entire mass of pseudoscientific jargon was thrown out. As pointed out earlier, the orthodox diffusionism to which he subscribed at this time places all cultural attributes on the same plane, collapsing diachrony into synchrony. This represents a key difference, if not complete incompatibility, with Marxism. The divorce was announced much later, however, and Lévi-Strauss would claim, with a touch of coyness, that he had always been a Marxist, but only minimally.[18]

Such considerations lead us very directly to the second text published here, devoted to Montaigne and, incidentally, to Jean de Léry. The circumstances are as follows. The talk was given in 1992, the anniversary of the "discovery" of America or, more specifically, as Lévi-Strauss liked to say, the discovery by one part of humanity of its other half. In any event, the period was, for Lévi-Strauss, one dominated by Montaigne (and Jean de Léry as well, to whom he has, ever since *Tristes Tropiques*, always recognized his debt). Lévi-Strauss had evoked the figure of Montaigne in *The Story of Lynx*, which closed the cycle of the *Mythologiques* and served as a kind of scientific testament for him. He gave the talk in the spring of 1992 and the following September wrote a piece for *La Repubblica* called "Montaigne et l'Amérique." In the space of a few months, therefore, Lévi-Strauss focused his thoughts on Montaigne. And it is striking to see that he didn't repeat himself, aside from his deep veneration for the man. In

The Story of Lynx, he addresses Montaigne's pessimism and remarks on the well-known statement in the *Essays*, "We have no communication with being" [*Essays*, 553], in other words, each of us constitutes a fortress of idiosyncrasies whose ramparts are habit and opinion. In the article he wrote for *La Repubblica*, we are given a very different reading of Montaigne. Knowing that Montaigne distinguished two modes of social life in America, that of the high plains of Mexico and Peru, quite similar to what once transpired in Europe in terms of complexity, and that of the small village units with an extremely loose political structure, he had already begun to question what was needed to forge the minimum social bond. In his 1992 talk, Lévi-Strauss reformulated this opposition in the terms of the time, by comparing "barbarians" and "savages." Of course Montaigne's genius lies in his ability to assign greater humanity to the second than to the first. Which amounts to saying that Montaigne would already have perceived the heuristic virtues of primitivism and that, intellectually armed in this way, he cleared a path for the lineage of political philosophy found in "Hobbes, Locke, and Rousseau" in the following centuries. And, of course, there was Montaigne's better known side as well, the voice of alterity, the man who was able to perceive the existence of humanities very different from our own. Because they participate in our world and enrich it through the spectacle they offer of themselves, they deserve our esteem and our respect. It is worth noting that this vision implies a fragmentation, a division of the human species, perfectly in keeping with the classical diffusionist premise. So, whether through its ode to primitivism or the apology for cultural diversity, the 1937 talk already confirmed the silent presence of Montaigne in Lévi-Strauss's thought.

The 1992 talk provides us with an abundance of intelligibility. Lévi-Strauss reminds us that Montaigne exercised caution in endorsing any kind of reformism. He would have understood that a society forms a coherent whole, and that if we try to change an element or aspect of it, we run the risk of dismantling it. In this sense, he would have been a "prophet" of functionalism, even structuralism in anthropology. Moreover, Lévi-Strauss could have added that Montaigne had already anticipated Marshall Sahlins's theory of the stone age as an age of abundance, having written in the "Apology for Raymond Sebond"[19] that

> these nations that we have just discovered to be so abundantly furnished with food and natural drink, without care or preparation, have now taught us that bread is not our only food, and that without plowing, our mother Nature had provided us in plenty with all we needed; indeed, as seems likely, more amply and richly than she does now that we have interpolated our artifice.[20]

The objective of this talk, which could easily be qualified as conversational, was not limited to cataloging Montaigne's many anticipations of anthropological thought. Rather, Lévi-Strauss went on to discuss Montaigne's sources with respect to the Americas. We are then engaged in a deeply erudite discussion involving a comparison of publication dates, considerations of the circulation of manuscripts before publication, and speculation on various readings, in order to answer a question that now seems to have been central for Lévi-Strauss: in his description of "Cannibals," does Montaigne rely primarily on André Thevet or Jean de Léry, on the Catholic or the Protestant?[21] At the time, the balance tilted in favor of the second, notwithstanding the Catholicism that Montaigne never renounced. And, after all, this is only right given that Léry's text is superior to that of Thevet, being more concise and emphasizing firsthand information over all else. In that sense, it anticipates the ethnographic method.[22]

Yet didn't Lévi-Strauss have something else in mind in choosing Léry over Thevet as Montaigne's preferred ethnographer? And in one of his last public appearances—although before a select audience who were amenable to his ideas—didn't the great anthropologist make a final attempt to identify the link that would secretly connect Montaigne to Rousseau?[23] And what would this link be other than the need for authenticity? But Protestantism, a religion shared both by Léry and Rousseau, a child of Geneva, could claim that need in the face of Catholicism, for which ceremony takes precedence in all circumstances. That link, no matter how tenuous, enabled Lévi-Strauss to articulate two radically different conceptions of alterity: an alterity of curiosity, which enriches the beings that we are, and a primary alterity, necessary for exchange, which results from renunciation and creates the fundamental social bond. These two forms of alterity demand the same intensity of approach, the same authenticity of self, even though the second operates at a deeper, more structural level than the first. In any event, Montaigne perfectly illustrates the first, Rousseau the second, and the mental universe of Lévi-Strauss, once he had discovered America and its Indians, never ceased to oscillate between them.

I'd like to conclude with a few words about Claude Lévi-Strauss's oral presentation. The two talks transcribed here, notwithstanding the many years that separate them, help us to perceive, to touch, almost to hear Lévi-Strauss's actual language. Its genius lies in the great proximity between speech and writing. A collection of letters sent to his parents during his youth illustrates this extraordinary verbal plasticity.[24] It's as if his writing was a continuation of his speech and his speech extended his writing. As if the respective virtues of writing and speech, precision on the one hand and rhetorical seduction on the other, were inseparable as a form of expression, and under all circumstances. The participants in his seminar remember this. Whether he was addressing the workers of the CGT or a circle of esteemed physicians, Lévi-Strauss always made himself accessible to his audience, always seemed to unsettle their beliefs. But if he was willing to lead them by the hand, he did so to better challenge their expectations. Additionally, his writings, even the most difficult, reveal an ongoing concern to keep the reader by his side, not to abandon him along the way. And he did this not by degrading his language but by making full use of it, that is, by becoming its servant. Lévi-Strauss falls at the opposite end of the spectrum from the many contemporary writers who write the way they speak and who speak like everyone else. He was the last classicist.

Ethnography

A Revolutionary Science

Claude Lévi-Strauss delivered this speech in Paris on January 29, 1937, to socialist and pacifist members of the Confédération générale de travail, a national trade union.

As Lefranc has just told you, we agreed, a few days ago, that I would speak today about ethnography as a revolutionary science. He referred to the difficulties of the subject, because the revolutionary nature of ethnography is, for me, something of a personal experience. I refer to ethnography as a revolutionary science because, after having fought for years in socialist organizations, my life has now become something completely different. I have been living among savage peoples, and what I have learned from that is that I haven't really changed my path, I continue to evolve in the same direction, regardless of the apparent distances and differences, which are immediately obvious, that these two aspects of my activity reveal.

In a way then there are two parts to my presentation.

But I should first say something about ethnography itself. This isn't difficult because you all know about it. You all know that an ethnographer is someone who goes to live among savages, who decides to engage with them in as friendly a manner as possible (which is not always easy) and who seeks to understand just about everything there is to know about their existence, their organization, and their way of life, and does so in relation to things that are very different from one another: how do the women go about making a ceramic vase, how do they handle the clay, how do they work it, how do they bake it—this is something that interests the ethnographer as much as understanding the religious beliefs of a people or their philosophical ideas about the universe—what methods do they use to catch fish, something that is as important for the ethnographer as knowing the terms employed to speak about oneself in these populations, what type of kinship relationships are there, how do they refer to an uncle, an aunt, a grandfather, a grandmother, or a cousin? In other words, everything that affects the life of the tribe under consideration, that is what the ethnographer studies.

Now, you'll say that these are quite modest and quite uninteresting concerns, and we, because we consider ourselves civilized, are not in the habit of worrying whether the buttons on a suit are on the right side or the left, assuming such savage peoples had suits with buttons.

But there is one thing I'd like to draw your attention to because it's one of the key elements of the problem. When we go about studying the history of a great country like England or Germany, we have at our disposal an entire array of works written, generation after generation, by men who were witnesses of what they are transmitting and have been able to provide us, through writing, with a faithful report. And through those accumulated and monumental writings, constituted by and for every people, the body of written documents about their existence, there takes shape a kind of comprehensive knowledge of the society under consideration. Consequently, there are a large number of questions that we don't have to ask about England, France, or Germany, because these are things that everyone knows from those many written documents that generation after generation has left to us.

Ethnography, however, works with populations whose most general characteristic, the most general feature they present, is that they do not possess writing, and when we encounter them face to face, we have at our disposal no document that would enable us to understand them. At that point, the least important objects they make use of, such as the rough pottery in which they cook soup or a feather that the men place haphazardly in their hair as an ornament, or a shapeless wooden weapon, are, for the ethnographer, precious documents because they are the only means at his disposal for penetrating, not only in the past but in the present, the life of the tribe he intends to study.

We have no books, we have no manuscripts, we have no written document, we have only rough, humble objects from which we must extract an understanding that historians can seek out in archives or libraries.

So, how do we do this and why do we do this? How do we go about working and what is so important about research of this type? That is the first part of my presentation: what is ethnography?

But the second part—in what way is ethnography itself a revolutionary science—is much more difficult.

There is nothing revolutionary about it in appearance,

for what is there in common between day-to-day political struggle and the detailed description of the way in which a fragment of [word missing] is made, for example?

On the other hand, we should be cautious of using the term "political" within a scientific study. We generally laugh at the idea that there could be a Marxist astronomy or a bourgeois mathematics. Aren't I taking a similar risk by speaking of ethnography as a revolutionary science? I don't think so, because the comparison is made somewhat spontaneously once we engage in ethnographic research. We find ourselves facing a number of problems I would call, in somewhat summary fashion, the problems of revolution.

From a historical point of view, it is remarkable that the progress we have made in understanding savage societies, in understanding backward or primitive peoples, has always corresponded to a development in revolutionary critique. I'll give you a few brief examples.

The first manifestation of the revolutionary spirit, by which I mean criticism applied to the institutions of the society in which one lives, is Greek skepticism. Its origins are extremely old and I don't want to retrace its history here. But Greek skepticism became a doctrine, a systematic school, at the exact same time as Alexander, in conquering the Indian subcontinent, placed Greek civilization face to face with cultures that were completely different from any it had known.

When, with the arrival of the Renaissance, a critical intellect reappeared in the West, for example, in the work of Montaigne, we find a clear correlation between the development of this critical faculty and the intellectual upheaval that occurred among sixteenth-century Europeans following the discovery of America. You know that the savages found in America hold a great place in Montaigne's thought. He refers to them frequently to illustrate the fact that notions of good and evil are relative, that social institutions can be viable even when they assume forms that are extremely different from those we are familiar with, that peoples who do not have the same religion or the same political status as us can live in a way that is fully harmonious and happy. And once this connection between the development of ethnographic knowledge and revolutionary critique was made, a permanent link was established. In every century you find, in the revolutionary literature, a systematic use of the new knowledge provided by the discovery of primitive peoples.

The sixteenth century is the century of the discovery of South America, and it is the South American savages whom you find everywhere in this literature.

But the eighteenth century brought us the penetration of North America, and you find the Indians of the United States in every line of prerevolutionary critique from the eighteenth century.

One final example to support my argument. The first years of the Russian revolution led to a remarkable development in ethnographic science in Russia. Indeed, it was only after the revolution of 1917 that we started to become familiar with the many primitive populations that exist within the confines of the Arctic Ocean or in the depths of Siberia.

Consequently, history itself assumed responsibility for expressing the problem: whenever the critical intellect regarding institutions tried to develop, it sought the example of savage peoples, and when a revolution occurred, it turned to those primitive peoples and those savages to deepen its understanding.

This is the historical aspect of the connection I want to make between revolutionary thought and ethnographic science. However, there are other considerations that also lead us to address the problem.

I have often heard some of my reactionary friends ridicule my interest in savage peoples. They say to me, "Your attitude is basically contradictory. You're a socialist and you're engaging in an essentially reactionary undertaking by attempting to defend and maintain civilizations that are more backward and much more undeveloped than our own."

The ethnographer is, indeed, a unique individual when on the left (and he is almost always on the left, as you will see): he is a man who attempts to critique the society in which he lives, to change it, to destroy its organization in order to replace it with something else; and, on the other hand, as soon as he is no longer in his own society but among savages, he becomes the worst conservative, the worst reactionary, attempting to protect those small tribes from the encroachment of civilization. A revolutionary in his society, he becomes a conservative among primitives. So that here too we have reason to consider the problem of the relationship between the ethnographer and revolution.

I would quickly like to clarify a few preliminary questions, questions of definition. These are always the most tedious, but they are necessary if we wish to continue.

We make use of a number of words to refer to those

who study savage peoples. We speak of anthropology, ethnology, and ethnography. I won't go into detail in making the necessary distinctions among these terms.

Ethnography is a very young science. It has just come into use. Depending on whether we are studying the physical culture of primitive peoples, or their social organization, or the anatomical structure of savages, we tend to use different terms. But this isn't very interesting.

What is more important is to define the term "primitive," which I have been using.

We are accustomed to saying that ethnographers study primitive societies. But what do we mean by primitive societies?

The history of the term is very old. We speak of primitive societies because, when America was discovered in the sixteenth century, we were convinced we had discovered absolutely primitive peoples. We had a very old tradition, dating from the Bible, according to which mankind, before becoming a society, lived in a golden age when there were neither social institutions nor philosophy nor industry nor anything that currently constitutes civilization. And when the first navigators arrived in America and found peoples who were naked, who had almost no industry, who had no knowledge of Christian Revelation, this legend of the classical golden age immediately assumed much greater solidity and strength. We thought we had rediscovered people who were the last witnesses of that legendary golden age. And from this the idea of "primitive peoples" arose, and it is with this understanding that we can employ it in these terms, not in the sense of absolutely primitive peoples, who don't exist.

But savages are relatively primitive peoples who represent a social state that is obviously not the first social state known to humanity but that is, nonetheless, something primary in the sense that it's a social state our societies would have known thousands and thousands of years ago.

This is another way of stating the problem, which may be appealing but is, I believe, dangerous. If it were true, we would have to admit that these savage peoples of Africa and America evolved much later than our own societies, that they are, in a sense, newcomers to humanity, that they are ten or twenty thousand years behind our societies, which would only make sense if they had come into existence much later.

It's an idea we merely have to examine to see its absurdity. When there were savages in the caves in the Dordogne, there were others already in America and Africa. The peoples we call primitive are as old as our civilized societies.

Maybe they evolved differently, the characteristics they display are not the same, but these characteristics are not more primitive than ours or, at least, are not necessarily more primitive than our own.

We are accustomed to thinking that humans and monkeys evolved from a common ancestor. But this doesn't mean that the monkey represents, with respect to mankind, a more primitive animal type than the human type, and anthropologists tell us that while monkeys may present a hundred characteristics that are genuinely primitive compared to analogous characteristics in man, they also present a hundred others that are, on the contrary, infinitely more evolved than those found in man.

Similarly, we are accustomed to thinking that the black race is primitive compared to the white race. It's true and it's false for, if Blacks possess some characteristics that are more primitive than corresponding characteristics in Whites, they have others that are more evolved. The development of the lips in Blacks is a much more evolved characteristic than the thin lips found in Europeans because it is absolutely certain that the remote ancestor common to Blacks and Whites was an individual with thin lips and not an individual with thick lips.

Whether looking at animal races or human societies, we find the same thing. We have different types that evolved differently, but there are many societies we call primitive and yet have social institutions that are much more refined and complicated than the social institutions in our own societies today.

But the word "primitive," when speaking of these peoples, has entered the language, and I'll continue to use it because we're accustomed to it and it's convenient, and because once we understand what it means, we can use it without fear of creating confusion.

What makes primitive societies different is that they are simpler than ours, which does not mean more backward or less advanced. This is a purely objective criterion.

First of all, these are small societies. Where European societies have millions and millions of individuals, primitive societies have thousands, hundreds, or sometimes dozens.

Second, technological activity in these societies is generally not very fully developed.

Nor are these societies very dense in the sense that

their population is scattered, which means that social phenomena appear to us with much greater simplicity than in our own societies.

In our societies, in order to understand a social institution such as the family, we're forced to examine a mass of documents and study a prodigious number of features, because our societies are dense and voluminous. But primitive societies, having small populations with low densities, display social phenomena much more readily, much more simply when investigated, than our own societies.

I'll give you an example to help clarify my thinking.

The phenomenon of digestion was studied in the oyster at a time when there was no knowledge about it in man. Now, the oyster is an animal much older than mankind, and it has, just like mankind, evolved over millennia. An oyster today is as different from an oyster of the tertiary period as we are from a primitive creature. But because it is a simple organism, it has been easier to study the phenomenon of digestion in this simple organism than in a complex organism.

The same holds true, more or less, for the study of social phenomena.

All of the difficulties encountered by the ethnographer come from a false understanding of the term "primitive." This is easy to understand. There was, in the mid-nineteenth century, a massive social upheaval with the appearance of theories of evolution. This brought about an undeniable sense of freedom compared to traditional metaphysics. The connection established, between mankind and the rest of the universe, the almost universal principle of intelligibility, whose value you are aware of and which we can no longer do without. At the time there was a strong temptation to extend this evolutionist explanation to all areas of human knowledge. We weren't satisfied with connecting human development with animal development, we felt that we could, perhaps, do something more and use this principle to understand the very different forms human institutions have assumed across time and space. Similarly, over an endless chain and through an unbroken series of intermediaries, we moved from current humanity to more primitive forms, then to simian forms, then from mammals to simpler organisms, and so on until we reached undifferentiated living matter. And we thought that it might be possible to connect our infinitely complex social institutions to increasingly simple institutions, which would enable us to make sense of the totality of human evolution.

To summarize, the evolutionist idea applied to human societies made two claims: first, that all human societies pass through a continuous series of stages by which they proceed from an extremely simple state to an increasingly complicated state; second—and this is considerably more serious and important than the first, given the consequences—that it is possible, by examining all the different forms of social institutions on the surface of the earth, across tribes and peoples, to reconstruct a chain, which would be the chain of human evolution on the social level. I'd add that if, on the surface of the earth, I find a people representing an institution that takes the form A, another of form B, another of form C, another of form D, and so on, I can construct a series A, B, C, D, representing humanity's evolution over increasingly complicated stages toward forms that increasingly resemble our current forms.

This is the point of view known as the theory of unilinear evolution, namely, that all human societies necessarily pass through the same stages and differ from one another only in terms of the stage in which they are currently found. So our society might be at stage Y or Z, whereas societies in India might be at stages M or N, and the tribes of Central Africa or Australia would be at stages B, C, or D.

It claims, on the one hand, that our society has necessarily passed through the stages we see today in societies in India, Africa, or Australia and, on the other hand, that those societies in India will themselves pass through the stages that will bring them closer to our own current state, that the indigenous people of Australia will necessarily pass through the stages that will bring them closer to societies in India, and then to current society.

I want to demonstrate how little support there is for this idea because it vitiates the development of the science of ethnography, our understanding of mankind, and the real revolutionary scope of ethnography.

So what is wrong with this idea? Human affairs are much more complicated than they appear to be when we first encounter them. Once we have carefully studied the thousands and tens of thousands of human types scattered across the globe, we see that it is very difficult to recognize stages in so many complex races. We've tried a number of approaches. At first we looked at technological criteria. We were told there are several stages: the age of cut stone, the age of polished stone, the Copper Age, the Bronze Age, the Iron Age; and by that principle, we attempted to organize all forms of social evolution. But that system collapsed entirely the day we realized that all of Africa went directly from the Stone Age to the Iron age, and that the Copper Age and the Bronze Age, aside from a few negligible exceptions, never existed. Consequently, this evolutionary law couldn't be applied to all societies in the world.

We then tried a different system. We were told mankind began as hunters, then became farmers, then herders, then industrialists. This system was somewhat more nuanced, somewhat more complex than the previous one. But once we had, instead of drawing conclusions from the vague narratives of travelers, studied the concrete existence of primitive peoples, we realized that the words "hunter," "farmer," "herder," were completely empty or, rather, in reality too full and contained such richness that they couldn't be used as categories.

Take hunting, for example. In principle, it's something very simple. But there are lots of ways of going hunting. There are peoples who hunted small animals with quite primitive means, such as a stick or stone made of jet, which they threw in the forest to kill small birds or small rodents; even insects were used as food. That was hunting.

But this has nothing in common with the highly complex hunting societies we find in Africa, where men armed with long-range bows hunt in groups to flush out, track, and kill large animals, such as elephants or lions, which is extremely difficult.[1]

It is obvious that these two conceptions of hunting correspond to societies that are completely different in structure and organization. In the first, social organization is extremely weak. Individuals work alone to find food for themselves and those close to them. In the hunt for large animals, however, even those that live in herds such as elephants or bison, there is need for a very solid social organization, given that hunting can only succeed through the collective effort of the entire tribe. So, to speak of hunting societies has no meaning at all.

Agriculture is exactly the same. There is an agriculture that consists, for the women of the tribe, in pulling up edible roots in the forest, then making holes near the hut and planting those edible roots so they will continue to grow and remain available without anyone having to travel to find them. Then there is an agriculture that consists in guiding a plow drawn by animals, thus an agriculture accompanied by livestock breeding and the domestication of those animals. Therefore, there are animals that need to be trained for this work and are no longer wild. Here, too, to speak of agricultural peoples has no meaning. In reality, there is no people that can be classified exclusively as a hunting, agricultural, or livestock-rearing society.

This led to subdivisions being made, and so we had agriculture 1, agriculture 2, agriculture 3, or hunting 1, hunting 2, hunting 3, corresponding to different methods of agriculture or hunting. But this shows how much more complicated it is than it appears to be. If men were hunters first, then farmers, they made a transition from hunting 1 to agriculture 1, which then disappeared, giving way to a completely different kind of agriculture.

But it is more complicated than that because, in primitive societies, men and women do not perform the same tasks, and engage in completely different economic activities. There are societies in which men devote themselves to hunting and women engage in agriculture; and there are neighboring societies where the opposite is the case, where hunting and agriculture are no longer the same and do not have the same numbers in the nomenclature of ethnography, so that we are faced with such a variety of facts, such a large number of differences, that it is absolutely impossible, from within all of this apparent confusion, to draw a dividing line. Every society embodies features that may not be found in a neighboring society. There are societies that make a direct transition from hunting to livestock farming, while others make the transition from hunting to agriculture without ever being exposed to livestock farming. Therefore, there is no way to apply these simplistic evolutionary criteria.

Yet these are not the most decisive arguments against this interpretation. Those come from the consideration of time and space.

When we think of evolution, we represent the evolution of humanity and have a tendency to imagine humanity in the form of a small baby who becomes a child, then an adolescent, and in this way is led toward maturity. We represent humanity as exhibiting the same continuity as the embryo that becomes a man or a woman, or the seed that grows into a plant.

In reality, things do not happen this way in human societies. I don't want to introduce too many technical concepts into this brief conversation, but all of you know that prehistorians, when discussing techniques for working stone, distinguish a number of shapes, each of which bears the name of the place where it was first discovered. The oldest evidence we possess of human industry is known as

Chellean industry, from a small village in Seine-et-Marne, near Paris. This industry is extremely coarse, consisting simply of taking a block of silex and reducing it until it takes on an ovoid shape with a pointed end. This can be used to strike or grind and is known as a "hand ax," because it is held in the closed hand and used without the aid of a handle.

To reduce a block of silex until it has cutting faces is one thing. And we might assume that nothing is simpler than to give it the shape of a pointed egg. But I would draw your attention to the fact that Chellean industry lasted approximately 100,000 years out of a minimum 125,000-year period during which prehistorians evaluate the minimal evolution of humanity, which is to say that throughout human development, which, in the minimal evolution model lasted 125,000 years, mankind spent 100,000 years repeating the exact same type of tool. Not only did mankind repeat the same tool identically during that time but also in space, because the objects of Chellean industry found in France are extremely similar to those found in Africa, and everywhere in Russia. For 100,000 years, mankind limited itself to repeating an extremely simple and coarse type of industry.

Then other industries appeared. It was learned, for example, that a more manageable instrument could be produced by using as raw material not a solid block but a flake, with a cutting surface, chipped from a block. This produced a knife, with which more could be done than with a hand ax.

These techniques and those derived from them were repeated until the discovery of metal, whose industry remained unchanged for three or four thousand years until the discovery of steam, and then electricity, by which humanity, in three hundred years, made greater strides than it had made during the first hundred thousand.

Humanity in no way resembles an infant who develops uniformly from birth to maturity, nor a seed that sprouts and grows into a tree. It is much more like an eighty-year old man who, for the first seventy years of his life, remains a child, unaware of the alphabet, and then from seventy to seventy-five years of age, goes to primary school and, finally, between seventy-five and eighty, advances to secondary and then higher education.

There is nothing that resembles continuous evolution. It is as if humanity was an inert substance and required some unexpected catalyst in order to move and change something about its condition.

The problem is determining why, when for a hundred thousand years mankind made do with an extremely rough-hewn instrument, it then required a more highly developed type of instrument.

This is one of the problems ethnography tries to answer, one that incorporates a multitude of factors and variants.

If humanity has a spontaneous tendency to evolve naturally, a social institution or technical achievement should form something highly typical once any human group is capable of assuming a given social configuration. When we look at the world map and the distribution of a technical achievement, we should find it distributed according to the laws of probability. However, that is not what happens. We do not find technical achievements or social institutions distributed throughout the world in this uniform fashion. They continuously occupy some spaces while being absent from others. A particular form of family organization, for example, will be consistently distributed across an area whose outlines can be mapped, whereas, nearby, it is completely absent. And a given technical achievement such as the piston bellows (a bellows in which the air, rather than being contained in a bag as in our civilizations, is pumped by pistons made out of bamboo sections) is found consistently distributed throughout the Pacific, from Polynesia to Madagascar, whereas east of Polynesia, in north or west Madagascar, this is not the case; the piston bellows has completely disappeared from areas adjacent to those in which it is prevalent.

The same is true of all the products of human science, all philosophies or religious beliefs, all technical creations, all forms of social organization, such as certain family structures, even certain forms of law. In some places they occupy entire regions, massive regions, while being completely absent from others.

Here we are presented with a particular phenomenon, which the ethnographer decides to study. I'd like now to briefly describe the subject matter the ethnographer studies.

About sixty years ago, the British anthropologist Edward Tylor gave us what has remained a classic definition when he said that the ethnographer's role is to study culture, which he defined as comprising all of the traditions, customs, methods, representations, and ideas associated with and characterizing a human society. It is a superficially vague definition but one that, in reality, has enormous significance.

What is the culture of modern French society? Well, it would be democratic and, at the same time, characterized by our habit of smoking paper cigarettes; it would be the parliamentary system and, at the same time, our habit of going to the movies; it would be the fact that a given religion predominates and that all the religions are monotheist and, at the same time, that there is a specific agency that picks up household garbage from the streets of Paris, and so on. This is an extremely broad collection of philosophical and religious ideas, technical methods, and habits. All of this constitutes culture.

Why make it a unified whole? Precisely because all of these phenomena, these manifestations of the life of human societies, have specific modes of behavior, which I would briefly like to define.

The intrinsic feature of a cultural area is that it occupies a given geographic area, is distributed continuously within a given perimeter. If we normally represent this perimeter as circular, this means that, barring any specific human or geographic difficulty, the cultural area will develop uniformly.

Of course, it is never circular in reality. The cultural area assumes a much more complicated shape. Some cultural areas, as among the Eskimo, have a very elongated distribution, with two strips of land to the south of the polar regions and to the north of America. But we can conceptualize it as a circular area, within which the cultural area can have two positions: a central position or a marginal position; and depending on which position it occupies, it will have completely different characteristics. In the center it is very rich and complex, it gives birth to a number of developments, of embellishments. At the margins, on the contrary, it is impoverished, weak, and sometimes there are only traces of its existence.

This can be illustrated with examples, and some rather striking examples, which are so impressive that they seem to have been invented to make a point.

American ethnographers have studied the development of a cultural area: ceramics in the southern United States. They found a central zone, A, containing ceramics with five colors; another zone, B, containing ceramics with four colors; a zone C, containing three colors; and so on, until there were no further signs of ceramics.

In similar fashion, they studied the distribution of small stone ornaments in northern New York. These ornaments had very different shapes, and they studied the regions in which the various shapes were found. Once again they found something similar: a zone where there were five types of ornaments, another where there were four, another where there were three, and so on, until there were no more ornaments.

At first glance, this suggests the idea that the zone with the most ornaments is the one where the ornaments originated, where a first type was initially created, let's call them square ornaments, and these square ornaments, originating in that location, had been borrowed, over the centuries, by neighboring peoples and in this way made their way in all different directions. A few centuries later, that same center began making round ornaments that followed the same path, and a few centuries later triangular ornaments; and so on. There comes a moment when America is discovered by the White Man. The first type of ornament, the oldest, has had the time to travel the farthest since its creation. The ornament that was created later travels a shorter distance. And so on, until we get to the last ornament, which doesn't travel beyond the area in which it originated.

This is only a hypothesis. But it was confirmed when excavations were made in the southern United States, the center of five-color ceramics, which were found in five layers, one on top of the other. The deepest layer contained ceramics with one color, exactly identical to the most distant zone; then they found the other ceramics in the other layers. In this way the hypothesis was confirmed: the five-color ceramics, which remained in the central region, were the most recent, the ones that didn't have the time to travel, whereas the others were so much older that they were found further from the site in which they were created.

This means that if we want to understand the phenomena of human culture, we must conceive of them not at all as phenomena that humanity somehow brings about spontaneously, as phenomena it carries with it as the seed carries within itself everything needed to make a tree, but we should consider cultural phenomena as developing at the surface of the earth exactly to the extent that they are borrowed. If the people of one area possess ceramics, it's because they borrowed them from the neighboring people, who had borrowed them from someone else, and so on. The same holds true in the case of square ornaments, round ornaments, or triangular ornaments, which reach them through a series of intermediaries from the site in which they were created.

You see how a human phenomenon of social organization or technical achievement can occupy broad regions of the surface of the globe, alongside other regions that show no signs of such developments. This means that alongside the people who created this social organization or technical achievement are others who have borrowed it, while a bit farther away are other peoples who have had no contact with the first group and who do not have the same characteristics. This doesn't mean they are at a stage that is too primitive but simply that their history has been such that they weren't in a position to borrow from the people who had developed that particular cultural area. I don't want to linger too long on this idea, but I'd like to conclude by discussing the implications of such a concept.

Its scope implies that we can, by this means, gradually reestablish the continuity of human history over many millennia, and that when we are in the presence of a primitive society, all of the objects it possesses, details about its technology, aspects of its beliefs, all of this helps make it intelligible and enables us to connect that primitive society to neighboring peoples with the same characteristics, only more advanced, who, therefore, were the initiators or, on the contrary, were more primitive and therefore the borrowers.

Until recently, our knowledge of mankind was limited to the features [displayed] by the great Western societies. If we turn to Africa or Asia or America, we are lost because we lack the means of investigation, because they are inaccessible. Ethnography established a method that allows us to integrate such extensive populations into history, such enormous portions of humanity that had once been completely excluded. Our study can help us better understand mankind.

So you see how I can claim that ethnography is also a revolutionary matter. To the extent that it helps us understand mankind it is so, and it is so also by showing us this diversity of beliefs, habits, and traditions that are the traditional link that has always closely connected a knowledge of primitive peoples with the critique of social institutions. And, finally, it is revolutionary in providing us with an extremely important lesson: to the extent that it is only by borrowing, by contact, that humanity's inherent inertia is broken, we can conclude that it is only when there are numerous contacts between peoples that social progress can be maintained and developed.

A few hundred years ago, on the plateaus of Central America, Mexican civilization was highly advanced.[2] It made great discoveries, erected monuments, had a social organization of the greatest complexity—and it collapsed when a handful of adventurers arrived from the shores of Spain. Why? Because Mexican society was isolated, had no contact with other peoples, and because it was completely handicapped by the arrival of representatives who were at the center of international exchange.

To the extent that the study of savage peoples shows us the intrinsic danger in which humanity finds itself, that it cannot move, advance, or change unless isolated and independent creations are exchanged from people to people; to the extent that it shows us that a society left to itself has no natural tendency to advance, that in order to awaken it to action, a multitude of small shocks resulting from contacts with other nations are needed; to that extent ethnography provides a lesson whose richness deepens the farther it travels to obtain its examples.

It shows us that this phenomenon is one that characterizes every individual small society, but because it studies very simple societies, it demonstrates that this phenomenon is characteristic of the very essence of humanity and that it is only to the extent that all the different centers of human culture make contact with one another that human and social progress can exist—and that isolated societies are inert societies and that societies must be in contact to advance.

I believe that this is the final conclusion that ethnographic studies will reach in the coming years, and it is to this that I wished to draw your attention this evening. [Applause].[3]

Return to Montaigne

Monique Lévi-Strauss, when asked, assured us that the following talk, one of her husband's last, took place in 1992. She stated that it corresponds to the indication "Doniger CP talk" written in Claude Lévi-Strauss's appointment book (which she kept) for April 9, 1992, at 5:00 p.m. Madame Lévi-Strauss recalled that she accompanied her husband and believes the talk was held in one of the rooms of the Paris School of Medicine. Our own research leads us to believe that it was given before the Comité protestant d'éthique.

During his presentation, Lévi-Strauss used lengthy quotations from Montaigne's Essays and Jean de Léry's History of a Voyage to the Land of Brazil. He used the version of Essays that is currently in print in the Livre de Poche series from Hachette. We used the 2001 edition, edited by Jean Céard. The quotations from Jean de Léry were taken from the 1880 edition by Paul Gaffarel, but the spelling has been modernized. Using these versions of two canonical texts, we were able to restore the continuity of a transcription that was occasionally incomplete.

It should be noted that the transcription was in parts corrupt. This required that, along with the essential spelling and typographic corrections, and the addition of a handful of missing words (indicated by the use of square brackets), specific modifications had to be made so that the meaning of Lévi-Strauss's words would be fully *available to the reader. Finally, the notes and title of the talk have been provided by the editor [or the translator, for citations relevant to the English translation].*

E. D.

[The beginning is missing] that is, chapter 31 of Book 1 of Montaigne's *Essays*, "Of Cannibals." In my talk I'll be using this text, which I hope we'll have the time to discuss.

This text—this chapter, rather—"Of Cannibals," is in fact part of a triptych, for [it balances] another text, another chapter, namely chapter 6 of Book III, which was written at a later date. We know that the first two books of the first edition of Montaigne's *Essays* appeared in 1580 and that Book III appeared only in later editions: in the edition of 1588, printed during Montaigne's lifetime, and in the 1595 edition, which came out after his death.

Chapter 6 of Book III is called "Of Coaches" and serves as a counterpart, which I'll discuss later. Where "Of Cannibals" takes Indians as its theme [a word is missing], that is, the representatives of the low culture of the tropical forest, "Of Coaches" is primarily devoted to the high cultures of Mexico and Peru. And both of these frame a third chapter, which serves as a more philosophical and moral reflection, in which Montaigne presents what are no longer his ethnological but his political beliefs, and that is chapter 22 of Book I, "Of Custom, and Not Easily Changing an Accepted Law."

During my brief introduction, I'll be moving back and forth between these three chapters; "Of Custom" will occupy a central position, flanked on either side by "Of Cannibals" and "Of Coaches."

As with many of the chapters in the *Essays*, "Of Cannibals" is constructed through a form of confrontation, tacking between classical texts and stories about antiquity and more recent records of personal experience.

Montaigne's point of departure is a group of quotes about the Greeks and Romans whose common theme is that when Greek, as well as Roman, armies confronted a non-Greek enemy, they referred to them as "barbarians." But when they saw the orderly formation of the adversary's troops on the field of battle, they said [finally]: "Why, there's nothing at all barbarous about this formation!"

Here Montaigne shifts almost immediately—this occurs in the second paragraph of the chapter—to more recent considerations, and here I'd like you to bear with me as I read from his text:

> I had with me for a long time a man who had lived for ten or twelve years in that other world which has been discovered in our century, in the place where Villegaignon landed, and which he called Antarctic France. This discovery of a boundless country seems worthy of consideration. I don't know if I can guarantee that some other discovery will not be made in the future, so many personages greater than ourselves having been mistaken about this one. I am afraid we have eyes bigger than our stomachs, and more curiosity than capacity. We embrace everything, but we clasp only wind.[1]

The action at once shifts to something very specific. Villegaignon, a French adventurer who went bankrupt in Brazil, a French colony at the time, had sailed with the blessing of Admiral de Coligny and the king, of course, in 1555.

We do not know the exact date when "Of Cannibals" was written, but we do know, more or less, that the first two books of the *Essays* were written between 1571 and 1580. So when Montaigne writes, "I had with me for a long time a man who had lived for ten or twelve years in that other world," it is highly likely that he's not referring to a companion of Villegaignon who left with him in 1555 but to someone who was already there. We also know that when the French first set foot in Brazil—that would be during Binot's voyage in 1504—there were a number of individuals, mostly from Normandy, who stayed behind.[2] These served as interpreters for the merchant vessels that landed to procure Brazilian wood or other raw materials, then considered precious. In fact, young men were sometimes imported and left with the Indians so that they might more easily learn the language and then later serve as interpreters or intermediaries. And almost certainly it was one of those interpreters who found himself in Montaigne's service, a man who had also lived in the area where Villegaignon landed, that is, the region of Rio de Janeiro.

The remainder of the paragraph, which may not appear to be very clear, becomes much more so when compared to a corresponding passage in chapter 6 of Book III, "Of Coaches," in which he begins the section devoted to the New World as follows:

Our world has just discovered another world (and who will guarantee us that it is the last of its brothers, since the daemons, the sibyls, and we ourselves have up to now been ignorant of this one?) no less great, full, and well-limbed than itself . . .[3]

This idea is always present in Montaigne's thoughts: another world has just been discovered, and might be the last, and occupies the other half of the world, [but], after all, we know nothing about it and it is certainly possible that there may be other worlds like this one that have not yet been discovered given the length of time we have been unaware of this other world.

[Yet] we can already see Montaigne lay out a number of arguments to show that it's highly unlikely that this New World, stretching to the North Pole in the north and the South Pole in the south, is a continent rather than an island, and that there is no more room available to the north or to the south, especially when we consider that the East Indies are quite near, on the other side, based on the belief that was held at the time.

He then engages in a number of considerations concerning whether this world could be the Atlantis described by Plato or some other marvelous world to which allusions are made in the ancient texts. And he sets aside such considerations for reasons we need not go into now, returning at once to his informant:

This man I had was a simple, crude fellow—a character fit to bear true witness; for clever people observe more things and more curiously, but they interpret them; and to lend weight and conviction to their interpretation, they cannot help altering history a little. They never show you things as they are, but bend and disguise them according to the way they have seen them; and to give credence to their judgment and attract you to it, they are prone to add something to their matter, to stretch it out and amplify it. We need a man either very honest, or so simple that he has not the stuff to build up false inventions and give them plausibility; and wedded to no theory. Such is my man; and besides this, he at various times brought sailors and merchants, whom he had known on that trip, to see me. So I content myself with his information, without inquiring what the cosmographers say about it.[4]

There are two points I'd like to make here: first, that this man wasn't Montaigne's only informant, and through him he was in contact with many other sailors or merchants who had been, so to speak, in the same region.

The second point, which is not immediately obvious, is that this is a barely veiled but rather pointed attack on a well-known author of the time. This was [André] Thevet, a Franciscan friar who had accompanied Villegaignon to Brazil in 1555 and had returned, most likely in 1557, and shortly after, in 1558, published *The Singularities of Antarctic France*. Thevet traveled a great deal: he spent nearly seventeen years away from France, from 1537 to 1554, and had been to the East and Middle East, especially the Holy Land. Villegaignon had taken him on as his chaplain and, also, to be the expedition's historiographer. His cosmographer, as well, which was the term used at the time. And in

1575 he went on to publish his *Cosmographie universelle*, in which he discusses Brazil on several occasions.

Yet Thevet, who was, apparently, a rather disagreeable man, did not hesitate to distort reality. For, ultimately, he was a kind of . . . let's say, an antiquary, a scholar, self-taught in some matters, a man who accumulated knowledge and let his opinions be known on everything and nothing. Now, very shortly after the publication of *The Singularities of Antarctic France*, Thevet was subjected to any number of criticisms. Montaigne doesn't list them here, but it is clear that the end of the last sentence, "without inquiring what the cosmographers say about it," very clearly has Thevet as its target. He goes on to say:

> We ought to have topographers [—not cosmographers, but topographers, that is to say, something much less ambitious—] who would give us an exact account of the places where they have been. But because they have over us the advantage of having seen Palestine [confirmation that he is referring to Thevet[5]], they want to enjoy the privilege of telling us news about all the rest of the world. I would like everyone to write what he knows, and as much as he knows, not only in this, but in all the other subjects; for a man may have some special knowledge and experience of the nature of a river or a fountain, who in other matters knows only what everybody knows. However, to circulate this little scrap of knowledge, he will undertake to write the whole of physics.[6]

—that is, to describe this small scrap [of reality] he will write all of physics in several large folio volumes.

It is extremely interesting to note that, at the time, between 1571 and 1580, let's say around 1575, there was considerable criticism of Thevet's knowledge of Brazil. In all likelihood, the interpreters, merchants, and sailors known by Montaigne had been as revolted by the 1558 publication of the *Singularities of Antarctic France* as Jean de Léry himself.

[The opening is missing] Léry, who had arrived in Brazil in 1557 (right about the time that Thevet was leaving) and left in 1558. However, he didn't publish his *History of a Voyage to the Land of Brazil* until 1578. Not only was the manuscript lost twice but Léry himself had been involved in all of the major religious disputes of the time: primarily the Saint-Bartholomew's massacre and the siege of Sancerre, of which he wrote a chronicle.[7]

We know that there was considerable hostility between Thevet and Léry, who accused each other of being an imposter. In fact, the entire preface of the second edition of Léry's *Voyage*, from 1580—the second edition, the first is from 1578—the entire preface is directed wholly and expressly against Thevet. But this was more than simply a quarrel between two ethnographers. And it is, moreover, amusing, based on the arguments they leveled at one another, to discover that their arguments are the same as those that might currently be expressed by our own colleagues when discussing similar subject matter: "He only stayed three months," says one. "No"—says the other—"I stayed there much longer, I went back." In that respect, it is absolutely modern.

Yet there is something much more serious here: a religious conflict. Thevet was Villegaignon's Catholic chaplain.

He accompanied him at a time when Villegaignon was himself a fervent Catholic. But we also know that Villegaignon had brought with him both Protestants and Catholics. In fact, Villegaignon's plan was to attempt to bring French settlers to distant lands, where it would be possible to put their religious disputes behind them and enable Catholics and Protestants to live in harmony.

But Villegaignon was having difficulty in Brazil. His head may have been a bit cloudy from the solitude, the strangeness, [and] the challenges, and he began having serious religious problems. After a while, he decided to write to Calvin to ask him to send a few Protestant pastors to help resolve the theological problems that were being hotly debated among this handful of French settlers in Brazil. So Calvin sent a few pastors, one of them being Jean de Léry.

This is more than a story about two ethnologists, it's a story about a Catholic and a Protestant who accuse one another of various misdeeds. There were serious problems in Villegaignon's colony: an insurrection, conflicts, executions. There were [even] plots against Villegaignon, who cruelly took revenge by executing the guilty. And there were mutual recriminations between Catholics and Protestants about responsibility.

In this context, it seems likely that Montaigne's local informers, who had seen what was going on, were hostile to Thevet and more likely to side with the Protestants than the Catholics.

I want to return to my text or, at least, to those parts of the text that are of interest here. And what I've found, to get back to my initial argument, the definition of barbarism, is the question that Montaigne raises at the beginning of his essay:

> Now, to return to my subject, I think there is nothing barbarous and savage in that nation, from what I have been told, except that each man calls barbarism whatever is not his own practice; for indeed it seems we have no other test of truth and reason than the example and pattern of the opinions and customs of the country we live in. *There* is always the perfect religion, the perfect government, the perfect and accomplished manners in all things. Those people are wild, just as we call wild the fruits that Nature has produced by herself and in her normal course; whereas really it is those that we have changed artificially and led astray from the common order, that we should rather call wild. The former retain alive and vigorous their genuine, their most useful and natural virtues and properties, which we have debased in the latter in adapting them to gratify our corrupted taste. And yet for all that, the savor and delicacy of some uncultivated fruits of those countries is quite as excellent, even to our taste, as that of our own. It is not reasonable that art should win the place of honor over our great and powerful mother Nature. We have so overloaded the beauty and richness of her works by our inventions that we have quite smothered her. Yet wherever her purity shines forth, she wonderfully puts to shame our vain and frivolous attempts.[8]

It is quite remarkable that Montaigne, in this passage—which is essential to our purposes—uses "savage" and "barbarous" as interchangeable terms, for, in the language of the time, savage and barbarous were not quite the same.

In what way do they differ? I would say that the difference is essentially political: savage nations are those very small nations that live in isolation from one another and do not seek to make contact with outsiders; whereas the barbarian nations consist of people who are capable of a degree of political organization and unity—even when they normally live in isolation—for the realization of large-scale undertakings.

I understand that confusion is needed for the purposes of his argument, so to speak, and that by constantly jumping back and forth and comparing ancient Greek and Roman texts with observations about the Brazilians, he makes use of the term barbarian for the first and, to relate them to the second, he has to establish some kind of correspondence between the two.

This is not the only place in Montaigne's text where this occurs. I'm thinking of the definition of savagery and barbarism. At the very beginning, he writes, "Thus we should beware of clinging to vulgar opinions, and judge things by reason's way, not by popular say."[9]

A few paragraphs later, in the text I have just read, he writes: "There is nothing barbarous and savage in that nation, from what I have been told, except that each man calls barbarism whatever is not his own practice."

And in this same essay he defines barbarism, or the barbarian, as:

> the one closest to natural law . . . All things, says Plato, are produced by nature, by fortune, or by art; the greatest

and most beautiful by one or the other of the first two, the least and most perfect by the last.

These nations, then seem to me barbarous in this sense, that they have fashioned very little by the human mind, and are still very close to their original natural-ness. The laws of nature still rule them, very little cor-rupted by ours; and they are in such a state of purity that I am sometimes vexed that they were unknown earlier, in the days when there were men able to judge them better than we.[10]

What a shame—says Montaigne—that Antiquity's great reformers, such as Lycurgus and Plato, didn't under-stand these people because, in all likelihood, rather than making their laws in the way they did and sending us in the wrong direction, they could have done otherwise.

Later he writes, "So we may well call these people barbarians, in respect to the rules of reason, but not in respect to ourselves, who surpass them in every kind of barbarity."[11]

A bit farther along in the essay: "Truly here are real savages"—here Montaigne returns to the word "savages"— "by our standards; for either they must be thoroughly so, or we must be; there is an amazing distance between their character and ours."[12]

And at the end of his essay, when he quotes a love song [*Divinemba*], which is an original document that we wouldn't have were it not for Montaigne, he writes, "there is nothing barbarous in this fancy."[13]

In the chapter "Of Custom, and Not Easily Changing

an Accepted Law," in Book I, we find another definition of barbary:

> Barbarians are no more marvelous to us than we are to them, nor for better cause; as everyone would admit if everyone knew how, after perusing these new examples, to reflect on his own and compare them sanely. Human reason is a tincture infused in about equal strength in all our opinions and ways, whatever their form: infinite in substance, infinite in diversity.[14]

And when we assemble all these texts, we notice that they do not exactly overlap and that we have, not always clearly but nevertheless recognizably, three different ways of defining savagery or barbarism. In Montaigne's thought they are sometimes explicit, sometimes latent. Each of them indicates one of the pathways that sociological or ethnological thought will later follow.

In its first formulation, the savage, what is savage, is that which is close to natural law, that is, which hasn't yet been adulterated. This appears very clearly in the passage where he writes, "Those people are wild [*sauvages*], just as we call wild the fruits that Nature has produced by herself and in her normal course; whereas really it is those that we have changed artificially and led astray from the common order, that we should rather call wild."[15]

Here we have a first sketch of what would later become the theory of the "good savage" found in Diderot and other writers.

In a second attempt, the concept of the savage applies

to any society evaluated according to reason. This comes out very clearly in the passage I have cited: "So we may well call these people barbarians, in respect to the rules of reason, but not in respect to ourselves, who surpass them in every kind of barbarity."

So, if following the criteria of reason, every society is barbarous, the problem immediately arises of the edification of a society unlike any that has existed and that would then, truly, be the rational society. If the first law leads us toward the theory of the "good savage," the second leads us toward construction of the social contract.

Finally, [there's] a third state of thought that comes through most clearly in chapter [8] of Book [II] and almost contradicts the previous idea, namely, that no society can be said to be barbarian according to the criteria of reason because all customs have their function, all customs have their purpose.

And I would again like to quote from chapter 23 of Book I: "Human reason is a tincture infused in about equal strength in all our opinions and ways, whatever their form: infinite in substance, infinite in diversity."[16]

Therefore, it's no longer reason that, in situating itself outside all social functions, judges them all to be indefensible or, in any case, indefensible for various reasons. On the contrary, it is reason that remains latent and underlies any type of belief or custom for which we can always find a justification. And, in the end, this will be Montaigne's political and moral doctrine as presented in "Of Custom" where, after an incredible presentation of what could be called an ethnographic documentation of all customs, after introducing the most contradictory quotations imaginable, for pages on end, one after the other, he demolishes them sequentially, showing that it is solely on the basis of where we are born and the education we have received that we believe something. The result is that all criticisms are absurd.

In fact, he adopts a practical attitude that is almost the opposite, for, where customs are concerned, we should maintain considerable, even complete freedom of judgment within but show complete respect without. That is the rule of rules and the law of laws that each of us must observe.

Why? And here I'd like to quote a text that is highly prophetic in the way it introduces contemporary functionalism, even structuralism: "It is very doubtful whether there can be such evident profit in changing an accepted law, of whatever sort it be, as there is harm in disturbing it; inasmuch as a government—that is, a social order[17]—is like a structure of different parts joined together in such a relation that it is impossible to budge one without the whole body feeling it."[18]

Therefore, a people's customs form a whole and it serves no purpose to criticize them, because if we criticize one, all of the others will collapse and, at that moment, a culture will collapse and we lose sight of its origin and evolution.

So, if the initial direction of Montaigne's thought leads to the theory of the noble savage, and the second would lead to the construction of a rational society from nothing, and to the Social Contract, then the third leads to integral cultural relativism. And in this we encounter the three cultures, the three ways of addressing problems in contemporary ethnological theories.

Obviously, much remains to be said about this chapter, especially the way Montaigne describes the savages of Brazil.

I would like to ascertain, out of a sense of thoroughness, whether it were possible that he was familiar with parts of Léry's manuscript—given that, as I mentioned, Léry's book didn't appear until 1578, two years before the publication of the first two books of the *Essays*. But because the manuscript circulated widely between 1560 and 1578, it's not at all inconceivable that, directly or indirectly, Montaigne had been able to obtain portions of Léry's text. I believe we can eliminate this possibility completely by examining various small details, and I'd like to provide one example: isn't it so, Montaigne claims, that the first man to show the Indians a horse "although"—he himself[19]—"had had dealings with them on several other trips, so horrified them in this posture that they shot him dead with arrows before they could recognize him."[20]

Léry himself is concerned about horses, but writes:

> I often wished while I was over there that our savages could see horses; but at that moment I wished more than ever that I myself had a good one between my legs. And indeed, I think that if they were to see one of our men of arms, well mounted and armed with a pistol in his hand, making his horse leap and wheel—if they could see the fire bursting out on one side and the fury of the man and the horse on the other—they would think on first sight that it was Aygnan—that is, in their language, the devil.[21]

Thus, Montaigne's informer refers to horses that are already present on the coast of Brazil, have already been introduced. For Léry, on the contrary, this is not the case, and from this point of view the facts are contradictory.

It is also striking to examine the way in which each of them speaks of the basic foodstuff of the Brazilian natives—manioc. "In place of bread," writes Montaigne, "they use a certain white substance like preserved coriander. I have tried it; it tastes sweet and a little flat."[22]

His "I have tried it" is very interesting. It demonstrates that the voyagers brought back with them certain foodstuffs [as well as] objects, because Montaigne states, in this same essay, "Of Cannibals": "There may be seen, including in my own house, specimens of their beds"—that is their hammocks[23]—"of their ropes, of their wooden swords and the bracelets with which they cover their wrists in combats, and of the big canes, open at one end, by whose sound they keep time in their dances," in other words, clubs. All of this goes to show that Montaigne already possessed an ethnographic collection.

But I want to return to the manioc and cannot resist quoting the entirely different text by Léry. It is worth quoting because it is like Proust's madeleine, which appeared for the first time in French literature:

This raw flour, like the white juice that comes out of it (of which I shall speak in a moment) has the fragrance of starch made of pure wheat soaked a long time in water, when it is still fresh and liquid. After I came back over here, whenever I happened to be in a place where starch was being made, the scent of it made me remember the odor one usually picks up in the savages' houses when they are making root flour.[24]

Note that the tone of the two authors is quite different; yet what is remarkably similar is their moral reaction to the so-called excess and barbarity of the savages, especially their cannibalism, which was a subject of much concern at the time.

Nevertheless, so that those who read these horrible things, practiced daily among these barbarous nations of the land of Brazil, may also think more carefully about the things that go on every day over here among us: In the first place, if you consider in all candor what our big usurers do . . . you will say that they are even more cruel than the savages I speak of. And that is why the prophet says that such men flay the skin of God's people, eat their flesh, break their bones and chop them in pieces as for the pot, and as flesh within the cauldron.

Furthermore, if it comes to the brutal action of really (as one says) chewing and devouring human flesh, have we not found people in these regions over here, even among those who bear the name of Christian, both in Italy and elsewhere, who, not content with having cruelly put to death their enemies, have been unable to slake their bloodthirst except by eating their livers and their hearts? I defer to the histories. And, without going further, what of France? (I am French, and it grieves me to say it.) During the bloody tragedy that began in Paris on the twenty-fourth of August 1572—for which

I do not accuse those who are not responsible—among other acts horrible to recount, which were perpetrated at that time throughout the kingdom, the fat of human bodies (which, in ways more barbarous than those of the savages, were butchered at Lyon after being pulled out of the Saône)—was it not publicly sold to the highest bidder? The livers, hearts, and other parts of those bodies—were they not eaten by the furious murderers, of whom Hell itself stands in horror?[25]

In the same way, but with greater truth, Montaigne writes:

I am not sorry that we noticed the barbarous horror of such acts, but I am heartily sorry that, judging their faults rightly, we should be so blind to our own. I think there is more barbarity in eating a man alive than in eating him dead; and in tearing by tortures and the rack a body still full of feeling, in roasting a man bit by bit, in having him bitten and mangled by dogs and swine (as we have not only read but seen within fresh memory, not among ancient enemies, but among neighbors and fellow citizens, and what is worse, on the pretext of piety and religion), than in roasting and eating him after he is dead.[26]

The source of the information is different but the way in which they respond is the same, and here as well we find an argument in support of a source, more Protestant than Catholic, of information about Brazil gathered by Léry.

Well, I think I've spoken long enough about this chapter and would like to leave a few minutes for discussion.

The title of the anonymous transcription is "*Conférence de M. Lévi-Strauss à propos du chapitre xxxi, livre I, des* Essais *de Montaigne: 'Des cannibales'*" ["Presentation by M. Lévi-Strauss on chapter 31, Book I of Montaigne's Essays: 'Of Cannibals'"]. A handwritten annotation has been added across the manuscript: "Pirated recording, uncorrected transcription."

Notes

Introduction

1. Emmanuel Loyer, *Claude Lévi-Strauss*, trans. Ninon Visonneau and Jonathon Magidoff (London: Polity, 2018).
2. The waters are by no means receded in France, where Lévi-Strauss is the object and motor of some of the most incisive thinking in philosophy and the human sciences. Apart from the readings of Philippe Descola and Eduardo Viveiros de Castro discussed here (the latter's *Cannibal Metaphysics* was first published in France), those of Claude Imbert in her *Lévi-Strauss: Le Passage du Nord-Ouest* (Paris: Éditions de L'Herne, 2012) and Patrice Maniglier's many essays stand out for their interpretations of the contemporary stakes of his thought, including his "L'humanisme interminable de Claude Lévi-Strauss," *Les Temps Modernes* 609: 216–41, and "Signs and Customs: Lévi-Strauss, Practical Philosopher," trans. Matthew H. Evans, *Common Knowledge* 22 (3): 415–30. See also Frédéric Keck, *Claude Lévi-Strauss: Une Introduction* (Paris: La Découverte, 2011); Vincent Debaene, *Far Afield: French Anthropology Between Science and Literature*, trans. Justin Izzo (Chicago: University of Chicago Press, 2014); Gildas Salmon, *Les Structures de l'Esprit: Myth en Lévi-Strauss* (Paris: Presses Universitares de France, 2013); and Pierre Charbonnier, *La Fin d'un Grand Partage* (Paris: Éditions CNRS, 2015). Maniglier's interpretation has had a strong influence on the orientation and content of the present essay, particularly with respect to the idea that there is an ontology of variation in Lévi-Strauss. See his *La Philosophie Qui Se Fait* (Paris: Les

Éditions du Cerf, 2019) for a briefing on his views on the anthropologist, including his case for "structuralism as a means of constructing an active, affirmative, and inventive relativism." (481) A major exception to the dearth of Anglophone readings is Boris Wiseman, *Lévi-Strauss, Anthropology, and Aesthetics* (Cambridge: Cambridge University Press, 2007). For a sympathetic and imaginative engagement with the person of Lévi-Strauss by a U.S. anthropologist, see Anand Pandian, *A Possible Anthropology: Methods for Uneasy Times* (Durham, N.C.: Duke University Press, 2019).

3. Lévi-Strauss apparently preferred "Mind in the Wild" to the eventual title the book received. See Loyer, 374. There is little reason to believe that "thought in the wild" is incompatible with the reappropriation of wildness by Jack Halberstam and Tavia Nyong'o in "Introduction: Theory in the Wild," *South Atlantic Quarterly,* 117 (3): 453–64. As Frédéric Keck recalls, "It is better to translate *la pensée sauvage* as 'wild thinking,' because the form of thinking that Lévi-Strauss describes is not limited to the mind of particular individuals called 'savages' but develops dynamically 'in the wild.'" See his "The Limits of Classification: Claude Lévi-Strauss and Mary Douglas," in Boris Wiseman, ed. *The Cambridge Companion to Lévi-Strauss* (Cambridge: Cambridge University Press, 2009), 141.

4. See Claude Lévi-Strauss, *Tristes Tropiques*, trans. John and Doreeen Weightman (New York: Penguin Books, 1973), 383–93, for the official account. See also "Jean-Jacques Rousseau, Founder of the Sciences of Man," in Claude Lévi-Strauss, *Structural Anthropology, Volume 2,* trans. Monique Layton (Chicago: University of Chicago Press, 1976), 33–43, for Lévi-Strauss's fuller, more subtle rendition of his views on the relationship between anthropology, philosophy, and Rousseau, including the latter's concepts of identification, compassion, animality and their bearing on the Cogito and collectivity.

5. "Amerindian dualism draws its inspiration [. . .] from an opening to the Other, an opening that manifested itself in a demonstrative manner during the first contact with Whites, even though these latter were driven by quite opposite motives."

Claude Lévi-Strauss, *The Story of Lynx*, trans. Catherine Tihanyi (Chicago: University of Chicago Press, 1995), xvii.

6. Certain major structuralists of a previous generation concur. See Marshall Sahlins, "On the Ontological Scheme of Beyond Nature and Culture," *HAU: The Journal of Ethnographic Theory* 4 (1): 281–90; and Terence Turner, "The Crisis of Late Structuralism. Perspectivism and Animism: Rethinking Culture, Nature, Spirit and Bodiliness," *Tipiti: Journal of the Society for Lowland South America* 7 (1).

7. For a summary from Viveiros de Castro's point of view, see Peter Skafish, "The Metaphysics of Extra-Moderns: On the Decolonization of Thought—A Conversation with Eduardo Viveiros de Castro," *Common Knowledge* 22 (3), 393–414.

8. See Philippe Descola, "Les Deux Natures de Lévi-Strauss," in Michel Izard, ed. *Claude Lévi-Strauss* (Paris: Éditions de l'Herne, 2004), 296–305.

9. It should be noted that Descola's account of how identification works is of more phenomenological than structuralist inspiration, in that he presumes rather than explains the identity of interiority and physicality with themselves (as his account of analogism reveals).

10. See the final chapter of *The Story of Lynx*, "The Bipartite Ideology of the Amerindians," 225–42.

11. See Eduardo Viveiros de Castro, *Cannibal Metaphysics*, trans. Peter Skafish (Minneapolis: Univocal Books, 2014), chapters 8 and 13. This is one of the points at which Lévi-Strauss and Strathern become compatible.

12. Lévi-Strauss, *Structural Anthropology, Volume 2*, 341.

13. Those are Lévi-Strauss's characterizations of China and Islam.

14. Lévi-Strauss, *Structural Anthropology, Volume 2*, 341.

15. That recognition is of course finally in quick decline, and with it must go the idea that anthropological concepts of relativism and alterity inevitably reinforce the authority of Euroamerican intellectuals—or else it will be difficult to reorient the "modern-centrism" of today's world.

16. Anabel Quijano, "Coloniality of Power, Eurocentrism, and Latin America," *Nepenthia* 1 (3): 533–80. It should be unsurprising

that an anthropologist engaged in cosmopolitics and the inter-
pretation of equivocations discovered that the straightforwardly
Marxist Quijano of the 1960s reduced indigenous politics in
Peru to peasant struggles—i.e., economic conflicts over "land."
See Marisol de la Cadeña, *Earth Beings* (Durham, N.C.: Duke
University Press, 2017).

17. Lévi-Strauss, *Structural Anthropology, Volume 2*, 307–8.
18. *Structural Anthropology*, 311.
19. The shift from Goethe to D'Arcy Thompson as the inspiration
    for the mode of transformation not only deprives structures of
    an original pattern but places the sorts of structural transforma-
    tions that myths undergo in living and nonliving beings, too.
20. Lévi-Strauss, *Tristes Tropiques*, 414. This is also the passage in
    which the self (*le soi*) is summarily dismissed as "detestable."
21. *Tristes Tropiques*, 414.
22. "Without deliberate intention on my part, a kind of 'mental
    tracking' shot has led me from central Brazil to southern Asia"
    Tristes Tropiques, 144. On French rationalism (and/or its Islamic
    counterpart) and Marxism (and/or Buddhism), see the final
    chapter of *Tristes Tropiques*, 405–415.
23. Foucault's unsigned essay "The Masked Philosopher" perfectly
    names his status as a thinker, as he elsewhere said, of philo-
    sophical fragments produced through human scientific means.
    "Anti-philosopher" is Alain Badiou's name for thinkers from
    St. Paul to Nietzsche and Lacan whom he regards as opposing
    their own singular discourse to truth in order to cure thought of
    philosophy.
24. Lévi-Strauss, *Structural Anthropology, Volume 2*, 22–23.
25. *Structural Anthropology*, 23.
26. *Structural Anthropology*, 23.
27. *Structural Anthropology*, 24.

Lévi-Strauss and the Diffusionist Moment

1. Lévi-Strauss continued to write, however. He was the author of a
   column that appeared in the Italian daily *La Repubblica* between

1989 and 2000. The French versions of these texts were collected and published in 2013 by Éditions du Seuil as *Nous sommes tous des cannibales* and, in English, as *We Are All Cannibals and Other Essays*, trans. Jane Marie Todd (New York City: Columbia University Press, 2016).

2. *Critique*, n. 540, May 1992, pp 374–390; reissued in Emmanuel Désveaux, *Au-delà du structuralisme. Six méditations sur Claude Lévi-Strauss* (Paris: Complexe, 2008).

3. Claude Lévi-Strauss, *Histoire de Lynx* (Paris: Plon, 1991). This appeared in English as *The Story of Lynx*, trans. Catherine Tihanyi (Chicago: University of Chicago Press, 1995).

4. Dina Dreyfus (1911–1999).

5. Emmanuelle Loyer, *Lévi-Strauss* (Paris: Flammarion, 2015), 177 and 132.

6. Denis Bertholet, *Claude Lévi-Strauss* (Paris: Plon, 2003), 84.

7. Grafton Elliot Smith, Bronislaw Malinowski, Herbert J. Spinden, and Alexander Goldenweiser, *Culture: The Diffusion Controversy* (New York: W. W. Norton, 1927).

8. Grafton Elliot Smith, in Smith et al., *Culture*, 12.

9. Herbert J. Spinden, in *Culture*, 12.

10. The Confédération générale du travail, founded in 1895, France's largest trade union organization.

11. Claude and Dina Lévi-Strauss were in Paris between December 1936 and March 1937. This brief absence from Brazil occurred between his sojourn among the Caduveo and Bororo (November 1933 to March 1936) and his work with the Nambikwara (May 1938 to January 1939). It provided an opportunity for him and his wife to present their collection of Bororo ethnographic objects at the Wildenstein gallery and for Lévi-Strauss himself to make a series of presentations, which are alluded to on page 281 of the French edition of *Tristes Tropiques* (New York: Penguin Books, 1992). See also Loyer, *Lévi-Strauss*, 192, which does not mention the talk reproduced here.

12. *Kulturkreise* would enter French manuals of anthropology in its original German form.

13. Alfred Gell, *Art and Agency: An Anthropological Theory* (Oxford: Clarendon Press, 1998).

14. Claude Lévi-Strauss, *Mythologiques*, volume 3, *The Origin of Table Manners*, trans. John and Doreen Weightman (London: Jonathan Cape, 1978).

15. Stith Thompson (1885–1976) continued the work of the Finn Antii Aarne (1867–1925), who sought to catalog the narrative themes found in myths and tales from around the world, and classify them into categories, subcategories, variants, and so on. The approach followed in the *Mythologiques* runs counter to this method.

16. This being said, the diffusionist temptation reappears nearly intact in *The Jealous Potter*, trans. Bénédicte Chorier (Chicago: University of Chicago Press, 1988), especially in the comparison between the fecal habits of the South American sloth and the strange way that the Californian demiurge had of relieving himself (pp. 203–205).

17. Lévi-Strauss, *Tristes Tropiques*, p 345.

18. Claude Lévi-Strauss (interview with Didier Eribon), *Conversations with Claude Lévi-Strauss* (Chicago: University of Chicago Press, 1991).

19. Marshall Sahlins, *Stone Age Economics* (New York: A. de Gruyter, 1972).

20. Michel de Montaigne, *The Complete Works*, trans. Donald M. Frame (New York: Everyman's Library, 2003), 406.

21. The dates of the first publication of André Thevet (*Singularities of Antarctic France*) and Jean de Léry (*History of a Voyage to the Land of Brazil*) are 1557 and 1578 respectively. The first edition of the *Essays* appeared in 1580, which left Montaigne little time to read Léry. Lévi-Strauss argues that Montaigne could have been familiar with Léry through a manuscript that would have been in private circulation before being printed, a practice that was common at the time. (It was because a text attracted broad interest and was widely circulated that a publisher invested money in printing it.)

22. Lévi-Strauss would go so far as to claim that the secret of Léry's ethnographic method "is that he put himself in the place of the Indians." In other words, he behaved exactly like a contemporary ethnologist. Claude Lévi-Strauss (interview with Dominique-Antoine Grisoni), "Sur Jean de Léry," in

Jean de Léry, *Histoire d'un voyage faict en la terre du Brésil* (1578), 2nd ed., 1580, text edited and with an introduction by Frank Lestringant (Paris: Le Livre de Poche, 1994), 11. [This interview does not appear in the English translation of Léry's book.—Trans.]

23. Most likely, this was the Comité protestant d'éthique, a group consisting mostly of physicians.

24. Claude Lévi-Strauss, *"Chers Tous deux": lettres à ses parents, 1931–1942* (Paris: Seuil, 2015).

Ethnography

1. The transcription uses the word "tiger," which we have taken the liberty to correct.

2. The transcription has the word "Africa," which we have taken the liberty to correct.

3. The following appears at the end of the transcript: "Stenography by O. Salafa, 2, boulevard Voltaire, Paris."

Return to Montaigne

1. [Michel de Montaigne, *The Complete Works*, trans. Donald M. Frame (New York: Everyman's Library, 2003), 182. All quotes from Montaigne are taken from this edition.—Trans.]

2. Binot Paulmier de Gonneville, captain of the *Espoir*.

3. [Montaigne, *Complete Works*, 842.—Trans.]

4. [*Complete Works*, 184.—Trans.]

5. Lévi-Strauss's commentary.

6. [Montaigne, *Complete Works*, 184–85.—Trans.]

7. *Histoire mémorable de la ville de Sancerre. Contenant les Entreprises, Siege, Approches, Bateries, Assuaus et autres efforts des assiegeants: les resistances, faits magnanimes, la famine extreme et delivrance notable des assiegez. Le nombre des coups de Canons par journees distinguees. Le catalogue des morts et blessez à la guerre, sont la fin du livre. Le tout fidelement recueilli sur le lieu, par Jean de Lery*, Genève, s.n., 1574.

8. [Montaigne, *Complete Works*, 185.—Trans.]

9. [*Complete Works*, 182.—Trans.]

10. [*Complete Works*, 185.—Trans.]

11. [*Complete Works*, 189.—Trans.]

12. [*Complete Works*, 192.—Trans.]

13. [*Complete Works*, 192.—Trans.]

14. [*Complete Works*, 96.—Trans.]

15. [*Complete Works*, 185.—Trans.]

16. [*Complete Works*, 96.—Trans.]

17. Added by the author.

18. [Montaigne, *Complete Works*, 104.—Trans.]

19. Added by the author.

20. [Montaigne, *Complete Works*, 186.—Trans.]

21. Jean de Léry, chapter 14. [See Jean de Léry, *History of a Voyage to the Land of Brazil, otherwise called America: containing the navigation and the remarkable things seen on the sea by the author; the behavior of Villegagnon in that country; the customs and strange ways of life of the American savages; together with the description of various animals, trees, plants, and other singular things completely unknown over here*; trans. Janet Whatley (Berkeley: University of California Press, 1992, copyright 1990), 118. Available at http://hdl.handle.net.i.ezproxy.nypl.org/2027/heb.03132.0001.001.—Trans.]

22. [Montaigne, *Complete Works*, 187.—Trans.]

23. Added by the author.

24. [de Léry, *History of a Voyage* chap. 9, 69.—Trans.]

25. [*History of a Voyage*, chap. 15, 131–32.—Trans.]

26. [Montaigne, *Complete Works*, 189.—Trans.]

Claude Lévi-Strauss (1908–2009) was a French anthropologist associated with the development of structuralism and structural anthropology. He was director of studies at the École pratique de hautes études at the University of Paris for more than twenty years and later held the chair of social anthropology at the Collège de France.

Emmanuel Désveaux is director of studies at the École des hautes études en sciences sociales.

Robert Bononno has translated works by Michel Foucault, Henri Lefebvre, Albert Memmi, and Isabelle Stengers, including *Speech Begins after Death* by Foucault (Minnesota, 2016) and *The Urban Revolution* by Lefebvre (Minnesota, 2003).

Peter Skafish directs the Institute of Speculative and Critical Inquiry and is the editor of *The Otherwise*. He has held research and teaching positions at the Collège de France; the University of California, Berkeley; and McGill University. He is the editor and translator of *Cannibal Metaphysics* by Eduardo Viveiros de Castro (Univocal/Minnesota, 2014).